BELOW THE CATARACTS

WRITTEN AND ILLUSTRATED WITH SIXTY PLATES IN COLOUR BY WALTER TYNDALE

PHILADELPHIA: J. B. LIPPINCOTT COMPANY
LONDON: WILLIAM HEINEMANN
1907

Printed in England

Illustrations reproduced by Hentschel-Colourtype

PREFACE

THIS book is the record of a painter who has spent some years of study and of work in the Nile valley. He has pondered long over the strange beauty of the Egyptian monuments; and if, either by illustration or description, he now succeeds in aiding others to an appreciation of the wonder and the mystery of these remains of a most ancient civilisation, and of the picturesqueness of life in Egypt to-day, he will not have painted nor written in vain.

The limits of space do not permit him to include in this volume all the interesting buildings of mediæval Cairo and of Pharaonic Egypt; and the temples of Esneh, Edfou and Kôm Ombo, though also situated below the first cataract, have been omitted, as it is intended to include them in a second volume, which will treat chiefly of the monuments above Thebes.

PREFACE

The author desires to thank those patrons of his art who have greatly assisted him by lending some of the paintings which are reproduced here ; and to acknowledge his indebtedness to M. Maspero, the distinguished head of the Antiquities Department, to Herr Bey and to Mr. Weigall, who have facilitated his work in the buildings which are under their supervision : and, indeed, to all the members of the different excavations, who have welcomed him to their camps, and have given him much valuable information.

CONTENTS

CONTENTS

LIST OF ILLUSTRATIONS

LIST OF ILLUSTRATIONS

LIST OF ILLUSTRATIONS

CHAPTER I

Port Said

As I revise these notes made during my last stay in Egypt, I read an announcement in the Press of a new line of English Turbine Steamers to Egypt ("The Egyptian Mail Steamship Co.") which will do the trip from Marseilles in three, from Naples in two, days. Things change quickly, for only last year I underwent no less than four days of boredom and biliousness between Brindisi and Port Said on a steamer that had to pass through the Suez Canal on its way to the Far East. There seemed to be no end to my discomfort, when I was suddenly awakened to the full consciousness of my existence by a remark, made half to himself by a fellow-passenger with his eye glued to a telescope,—"Yes, that is Egypt right enough." I soon satisfied myself that his eye needed a rest, and, begging leave to have a peep myself, with trembling fingers I adjusted the focus till the low-lying coast of Egypt was plainly visible.

The coast lengthened visibly, for what at first looked like two islands proved to be one piece, as a yet more distant bit of land gradually came into sight. This long line of coast then seemed to disintegrate, form itself into islands, disappear, and be picked up again far to the west. By referring to the map these changes were explained, for the whole coast of the Delta, except in one or two places, is but a narrow strip of land separating the great salt lakes from the Mediterranean.

The aimless pacing up and down the deck, and the various attempts one makes to kill time, had now come to an end. Grey wintry skies and troubled waters were left far behind us; the sun shone benignly down from a soft blue expanse, and the gentlest of summer breezes imparted an inspiriting freshness to the dry, warm air.

The great steamer ploughed its rapid way through the yellowish-green water opposite the mouth of the Nile; then, away to our right, a low-lying, golden sand-marsh outstretched itself, and now, far ahead, the outline of a lighthouse and the masts of many ships came into view.

Presently, extending itself towards us through the water, a long, grey line appeared, which, as we approached, resolved itself into a huge length of breakwater; and, beyond it, upon our right hand, the confused outline of houses, of a town, grew gradually clear.

Slowly, and yet slower, the steamer glided along, until, amid many peremptory orders from the captain's bridge, much shouting and running to and fro of Lascars, and excited preparation on the part of passengers, the engines ceased working, the great anchor was slowly dropped, and our vessel settled into her berth in the still waters of the harbour of Port Said.

It was a thrilling moment to a new-comer! There, there, across the pale, shining sands, lay Egypt—the land of the Mysterious River, the magic country of one's longing dreams. The land of mosque and minaret, of turban and of yashmak, of Pharaoh and pyramid and sphinx, of desert and of camel: the old, old land of wonder, of strange, weird mysteries; perplexing tokens left from the days when the world was young—enduring there in the golden sand beside the grand old river—a heritage from the dawn of the ages.

The still water of the harbour was of a pale, greenish hue, and so marvellously clear that one could watch the gliding jelly-fishes far below the surface—wonderful jelly-fishes, resembling huge button-mushrooms, of a beautiful, heliotrope transparency, with long streamers floating out beyond them. Away across the marshes to our right the sun was now setting in serenest splendour. Not a fleck of cloud upon the sky, but, above us, the most gloriously pure tints of azure, which, towards the west, imperceptibly toned into faint green, fainter aquamarine, and pale lemon, and then was merged into a wealth of golden splendour; the whole indescribably calm, clear and majestic in effect.

"Oh, East is East, and West is West, and never the twain shall meet."

Even here upon the water, ere ever we had landed, all was strange and picturesque. Scarcely had our ship settled herself into place before a score of small boats clustered round her, filled with eager, gesticulating natives, with goods for barter; fruit and cigars, beads and feathers; others bringing boys, who, for few pence, would make wondrous dives beneath the ship, appearing a moment later, with white teeth all agleam, on the other side of the great vessel. In one boat the rowers were chanting a native air from which a once-popular London music-hall refrain was taken, "Ta-ra-ra-boom de aye!" How familiar, and yet how strange, heard here, in these surroundings.

Then, gliding ominously towards us in the evening light, came a string of broad barges, black, black, from stem to stern; bearing black cargo, and all alive with moving, chattering black atoms, looking like doomed creatures from the nether world—the coal barges, already on their way to replenish the dark, yawning cavern in our vessel's midst, with food for the mighty monster lurking there, whose fiercely throbbing heart was stilled for a space.

Their advent meant the closing of the port-holes and doors of the ship, to exclude, as far as possible, the all-penetrating coal dust; so we hastened to collect our belongings and to steer our course in the direction of the gangway, for it was now necessary to prepare to put foot on the shore of Egypt. However much one might wish to indulge in the delightful sensations that arriving in a new country conjure up, it was now only at odd moments that one could do so, for boatmen, porters, custom-house officers, and hotel touts have little respect for sentiment, and insist on claiming most of one's attention. Messrs. Cook and Son have done much to mitigate this evil, and save the new-comer a great deal of worry and expense, but until certain formalities have been gone through one is compelled to drop the Egypt of the Past and content oneself with the Egypt of the Present. I was well aware that Port Said was not a place for a painter to loiter in, so I made up my mind not to consider it as a part of Egypt, but merely as a European excrescence, and decided to clear out as soon as the first Cairo train left.

A good deal of the journey to the capital was through a hungry-looking country, with the partially drained lake of Menzaleh to the right and the Arabian desert to the left, and the Suez Canal in the immediate foreground. It seemed as though one was never to lose sight of this canal, and its important bearings on commerce and politics failed to compensate me for its ugliness. But I partially succeeded in blotting it out of sight by sitting very low down on the seat, bringing the window-sill just below my horizon.

There was much to enjoy beyond. The long stretches of desert which connect Egypt with the Sinai Peninsula have a peculiar charm of their own; it was, moreover, my first sight of the desert, and though, since then, I have spent months in the wilderness, and seen it in all its aspects, that first sight of it still stands out clearly in my memory. Imagination was fired. This was probably the first sight the child Jesus saw when Mary and Joseph made their pilgrimage into Egypt to seek refuge from the wrath of Herod. At what point did they cross the track which I was travelling? Did Mary look like that fellah woman riding to the station on a donkey? The dress she wore had altered little in shape in the past two thousand years. The shawl that partially hid her face was also a wrapping for a babe which she carried in her arms. As they approached, some chance movement of the child drew the veil from its mother's face, and, alas, the illusion was gone!

Some ten years later I was again going to Cairo by this route; the steam tramway that formerly took us as far as Ismailia had given place to a well laid line, with trains running Pullman cars, restaurant, &c., &c. Some ugly erection here and there, and a few advertisements, were the only other signs I noticed of the increased prosperity of the country. I could have dispensed with the latter, but I was thankful to be able to do the journey in about half the former time; for the heat was intense, and, owing to a stoppage in the Suez Canal, the train was very crowded.

Though the landscape to the right of me was apparently unchanged, I was amazed at the altered appearance of the desert on my left. Where I remembered seeing but an arid waste I now beheld great stretches of water, with islands and palm groves. It certainly was the time of the high Nile, but I was sure that its waters could not reach so great a distance. I consulted my map, and got little help from that; but on asking a native who was sitting near me whether there was always water in that direction, he answered, "Mirage." Never before had I seen this phenomenon in so realistic a manner, and, wishing to share my joy with some steamer acquaintances who were in another compartment, I hurried off to point this out to them. A careless "Oh, indeed!" from some of the fair sex, and a question from one of the men as to whether I could tell him "the exact width of the canal," hurried me back to my part of the train.

Pulling up, later on, at a commonplace little station, the guard calling out "Tel-el-Kebir" was rather startling, but I did not attempt to share my emotions with my unsympathetic friends of the mirage.

Not before reaching Zakâzîk does one fully realise that one is in the Delta, where one recalls the saying of Herodotus, "Egypt is the gift of the river"; for though the Nile itself is not seen till the train nears Beulia, its influence is felt everywhere. Some of the landscape is very fine; well wooded, with picturesque water-courses. The ruins of Bubastis are near Zakâzîk; these were excavated by Professor Naville some twenty years ago, but though of considerable archæological interest, their pictorial aspect hardly repays a visit. Bûlâk looks disappointing from the railway station, and being within such easy reach of Cairo one is loath to break the journey. In another twenty minutes or so, looking out to the right of the way you are travelling, you will catch your first glimpse of the Gizeh Pyramids. Seen at this distance it is hard to realise their size, and although I was neither disappointed nor the reverse, I felt my heart beating faster ; and had the railway guard asked for one more clip at my ticket at that moment, I might have become dangerous. The train rushes on. The Delta now visibly contracts; the two ranges of hills that enclose the Nile valley come into sight, the Mosque of Mohammed Ali, which crowns the citadel, looms in the distance, and you realise that your journey is coming to an end.

CHAPTER II

Masr el Kahira

Should any of my readers, arriving in Cairo for the first time, imagine, as I did, that they will at once drop into a city saturated with the spirit of the East, they will feel the same disappointment as myself, and a word of comfort may not be out of place here. The drive from the station to any of the hotels is through a part of Cairo that is no more like the Masr el Kahira painted by Lewis, or described by Lane or Amelia B. Edwards, than Peckham resembles Pekin. Hardly a house that we see here existed forty years ago ; and, from the look of them, they may tumble down before another forty years elapse. The builders of these erections had beautiful models near at hand to inspire them ; but that fatal "L'Egypte fait partie de l'Europe" of Ismail Pasha turned their attention to Paris, and now we have a shoddy imitation of that capital, with here and there some erection run up "en style Arabe" or "en style

Egyptien," or, worse still, "l'art nouveau" as understood by the Levantine architect. You will find your hotel "replete with every modern comfort," as the advertisements have it—and your bill proportionately high—but with very little characteristically Eastern about the place, beyond a few bad reproductions of some of the temple wall paintings, and some waiters dressed in a garment which looks like a night-shirt, girt about with a red sash, and the nearest imitation to a flower-pot on their heads; features which may or may not assist you to realise that you have come to one of the most picturesque cities in the world. Take comfort, however, and look forward to a stroll round the old town on the morrow, which, if you are in search of the oriental and the beautiful, will exceed all your expectations. Indeed, the mile or two that separate your hotel from the Khân Khalîl seem to separate the East from the West, in everything but climate.

Much has been improved away since my first visit; the canal that crossed the old city from north to south—El Khalîg, as it is still called—is now filled in, and an electric tramway runs along it; many a Meshrebiya window is now replaced by sashes made in Sweden, and a good number of old houses have either been pulled down or else modernised out of all recognition; but still so much remains to incite the imagination, and to make one long to set up one's easel, that it is better not to indulge in vain regrets.

Starting from the Ezbekiyeh, which is the centre of the European quarter, an uninteresting little street behind the Bristol Hotel will lead you through a labyrinth of lanes and alleys into the Suk ez Zalat. You will do well to have a guide, for already the rectangular plan of the modern town has ceased, and the streets turn and twist about, with a knack of ending nowhere, in the characteristic way of an oriental city. This first part of your exploration is through a disreputable quarter indeed ; for here all that is squalidly vicious in Europe and the near East flourishes ; but it is quiet enough in the morning, when the least desirable inhabitants are still sleeping off the orgies of the previous night.

Once safely landed in the Fouyatieh and you will have left Cairo improper behind you and will really be getting into Cairo proper. A mosque and a row of lattice-windowed houses to the right might serve as a setting to some Arabian Night's story. An unpretentious-looking doorway, shadowed by the projecting upper floor and ponderous bay windows, leads into the courtyard of a typical Cairene house, once inhabited by some wealthy merchant, but now let out in tenements.

Should you be fortunate enough to hap upon a guide who has been used to conducting artists, he will be able to show you many such houses ; and I may here mention the name of one who has followed the writer, in his search for the picturesque, into every hole and corner of Cairo. His name is " Mohammed el Asmar," but he elects to call himself "Mohammed Brown," the latter name being a literal translation of " Asmar " ; " besides, am I not brown ? " he argued, in justification of his change of surname. With the aid of Mohammed I used this court-yard as an outdoor studio for some time, he being able to procure me water-carriers, sellers of sherbet and other drinks, donkeys, camels, and all the other living objects of interest of a Cairo street. While he haggled and bargained with my models, I was able to make studies of the arabesque door and the pretty bits of Meshrebiya seats which I hope have not now gone the way of so much that is picturesque.

Meshrebiya is the Arabic name for the turned woodwork that was so much used for screens, lattice windows, and furniture generally ; it admits the air, subdues the light, and also allows the women-folk to get a peep into the outside world without their being seen. This is well in keeping, in a Mohammedan town, where shade and privacy are essentials, but taken away from its surroundings, and set up in some suburban villa at home, it appears singularly out of place. Tons of this woodwork have been bought by dealers, and sold to tourists to be made up into draughty screens, summer houses, and even picture-frames, which are all doomed to be cast aside later, when the unfortunate purchaser has fully realised the unsuitableness of his bargain. I know of one case where the woodwork of a fine old Cairene house has been rotting in a barn in Surrey ever since the despoiler brought it to England some forty years ago. Struck by its beauty when he saw it in its proper surroundings, he hoped that his architect would be able to make use of it for a house he was about to build; but the sunlight of Surrey could not stand such an amount of subduing; the Nordracht treatment had not then brought draughts into fashion; nor did his women-folk see the necessity for hiding their pretty faces behind the lattice.

The regrettable part is that this old woodwork is never replaced in Cairo, for, as the houses in the older parts of the city do not repay their owners, the drainage has been shockingly neglected, and those who can afford it clear out and build some bastard-looking modern house in the newer quarters.

Let us continue our walk along the Suk ez

W. Tyndale

Zalat. The sights become more bewildering as we get nearer the heart of the city ; and as the street narrows so the noise increases. Camels move slowly along, quite indifferent to the excitable cabmen, who may be cursing the shades of their fathers because they do not get out of the way; the man with the long-bodied and seatless donkey-cart that still does duty as an omnibus joins in the clamour; "May your women-folk only bear pigs!" he yells out to the camel-driver, and should the block become apparently hopeless, advice is shouted out by most of the onlookers, while some jest from a donkey-boy who has managed to squeeze his beast through sets the crowd laughing. Then, somehow, the camels manage to move on, with an expression of supreme contempt for the curses, jeers and jests that have been showered upon them and their drivers.

As the sun gets higher in the heavens the strip of shade narrows on the north-eastern side of the Suk, and before one reaches the end of this long street the tradesmen have let down their awnings upon each side of the road. It is a relief to turn the corner and not to face the sun for a while.

El Nahassin is now reached, and while the life and bustle are as picturesque as ever, the beauty increases, for soon, on the right-hand side, we see the domes and minarets of the group of mosques that surround the Muristan. The Sebîl Abd er Rahmân, on the left where the roads widens, is a good place from which to enjoy this view ; it is at the bifurcation of the two streets, thus permitting you to stand and look down the centre of this highway, which it is often difficult to do, now that the traffic is so much congested by the free use of European cabs.

The various " Sebîls " are a characteristic feature of Cairo. Formerly the chief water supply, they are still used as drinking fountains. They are maintained out of the religious endowments, and are nearly always surmounted by a class-room, from the open windows of which the sing-song of the children learning their Koran comes wafted down to you.

The steps of this particular Sebîl form a good vantage ground from which to make a sketch of this fascinating scene. A dingy old palace is on your left, and the houses beyond, on each side of the street, are being left to crumble away in peace. Where the Meshrebiya of the windows has gone in places, an old piece of sacking " stops a hole to keep the wind away," and the charming bit of fret-work that forms the curtain of the bay hangs here and there by a thread, until it makes up its mind which turbaned head it will descend upon. These signs of decay may be seen in many a

Continental town, where the street is grass-grown and silent, but here the contrast is startling; the road is crowded, and on the ground floor of each house someone is either busy plying his trade or enticing customers to buy his wares. Nothing seems to be done indoors; food is hawked about and eaten in the shade in summer, and on any sunny doorstep in winter; men sit smoking their narghilehs and sipping their coffee outside the coffee-house, for the inside is often but a box with barely room for the host to cater for his clientèle; the barber will shave the head, or possibly bleed, or draw the tooth of a patient, either at his doorway or on a bench outside; the scribe will sit in the open to draw up a deed, to write a love-letter for some veiled young woman squatting near him, or to bear witness to a bargain struck by a fellah and some townsman. Privacy is only a matter of sex. The donkey-boy will beat his wife should she cross the road unveiled, but his father may have haggled for weeks over the sum to be paid for his daughter-in-law, with an inquisitive crowd around listening and commenting on every detail.

This being a part of the main artery of the city, running from the north to the south, the traffic is often considerable, and it is a keen delight to watch this pass, in all its colour and picturesqueness, before a long familiarity with it has caused one to forget the drabness and gloom of a crowd in a London street.

Let us now move on. What a grand old house is this to the right! While you are admiring it an old Sheykh opens a lattice window and calls out the hour of prayer; and from every minaret, in either soft or loud, high-pitched or deep, sonorous voice, do you hear the cry of the muezzin, "Lâ ilâha ill'allah, wa Muhamed rasul allah." On a Friday the faithful will often close their shutters, and hurry off with their customers to join the "Duhr," or midday prayer. But why should the muezzin call from this wonderful looking house? This puzzled me a good deal while I was sitting in the little café opposite painting my sketch. The faithful Mohammed Brown, who had hitherto sat near me to keep off the small boys and flies, hurriedly asked the landlord to keep an eye on me, ran across the road, took his shoes off, and disappeared through the portal, to return some twenty minutes later with an apology for leaving me so abruptly; he had quite forgotten that it was Friday till he heard the call to prayer, and it was all he could do to get through his ablutions in time to join in the "Duhr." I discovered then that the subject of my sketch was a mosque, with the sheykh's house built alongside and above the porch, the original

building being so hidden from the street that the muezzin had to shout from the sheykh's bedroom window. The way the architect managed to fit this dwelling on to the original building is wonderful. A good deal of the ornamental woodwork has disappeared, but enough remains to make it one of the most picturesque bits in Cairo. That there should be a little café hidden away in the archway opposite, making a safe place from which to sketch it, was a matter for self-congratulation. To get another view of it, with the group of mosques beyond, I had to make a bargain with a vendor of goads and walking-sticks to allow me to sit on his counter. After much haggling, Mohammed got me this concession for five shillings, and it was arranged that I might monopolise the vendor's counter for five consecutive days. He insisted on being paid in advance, which I thought was suspicious; however, witnesses to the payment were procured from the café, so I decided to risk it. All that morning my vendor of goads sat rather nearer to me than I liked; but, on arriving there the next day, I found the shutters up, and concluded that I had been done. A neighbouring shopman after a while informed us that Mustapha of the goads had left the key of his shop at the café, with a message that his counter was mine for a whole week, while he was visiting some relations in the country. "After all," said the neighbour, "his counter is bringing him in more now than when he was keeping shop, for the trade in sticks generally is very slack now; and he has not seen his people for some years."

We now pass the mosque of Sultan Barkuk, pausing to notice its marble portal and bronze-mounted door next the Tomb-mosque of Mohammed en Nasr, which joins the Mûristan, or hospital, built by Sultan el Mansur Kalaûn during the latter part of the thirteenth century. This great Mamlûk Sultan built and endowed this hospital as a thank-offering after being cured of a dangerous illness. His mosque and tomb adjoin it. We shall refer to this beautiful group of buildings later on.

Should the reader be an old traveller he will need no advice from me, and can skip this page; but should he find himself in the East for the first time, and not be attempting to do the whole of Egypt during a Christmas holiday, I should recommend him to spread his sight-seeing over a good many more days than most guide-books allot to it. The bored look of the tourists as they are being rushed from place to place, and their expression of dismay when told of one more thing they *must* see before returning to the hotel, justifies me in holding the view that the art of enjoying travel is only partially understood. Treat your mind and your eyes with as much respect as you would treat your stomach, only attempting to see as much in one day as you can enjoy and digest, and you will carry away much pleasanter and more lasting recollections of your holiday. To watch the life in the streets, the various trades that are plied within sight of all, the wares displayed in shops and bazaars, the strange costumes of the men and women buying and selling, lolling about in the sun in winter, or squatting in groups in summer wherever an awning or porch casts a shadow—this is surely as much as one can enjoy in a morning.

CHAPTER III

In The Bazaars

Around the Mûristan we realise more than at any other point in this long thoroughfare that we are in the "Nahâssîn," or coppersmiths' market. Hitherto we have seen many other goods made and laid out for sale, to wit, the wares of our friend of the goads, but here the coppersmith's craft holds its sway as in days of old. Strange vessels are still being hammered into shapes that might have adorned Haroun al Raschid's kitchen dresser. It is consoling to reflect that this is still a living handicraft, that these coffee-pots and kettles should still have retained their beautiful forms, and are being made by Cairene craftsmen, to be bought by the natives, and not merely displayed to tempt some tourist. As a matter of fact, I have never seen one of these being sold to the "Firangi." They are too bulky, perhaps, to pack away in a portmanteau, or may be the smith and dragoman have not been able to come to terms as to the commission the latter is

to get out of a purchase. The stalls that a few years ago stood at the base of two of the mosques here have now been cleared away, with a certain loss to the picturesqueness of the scene.

Further on, a narrow turning on your right leads into the goldsmiths' bazaar. The several alleys which one passes through before one emerges again into the main thoroughfare are here so narrow as not to admit of two people walking abreast; the shops are mere open cupboards with a frontage of three or four feet; the floor is raised about two feet, and forms a seat for the customer. This little box of a place serves as workshop and show-room; the "guhargi" or jeweller squats here all day cross-legged, and need hardly move from his position, as all his goods are within easy reach, and his cup of coffee or green tea is brought to him in answer to a clap of his hands. His type of countenance differs little from that of his neighbours in the Nahâssîn, but a slight difference in his dress tells you that he is not a follower of the Prophet. On Saturdays you will find most of these shops closed, and if you can decipher the names over the locked doors you will find neither that of "Hassan" nor "Mohamed," but "Ibn Yusef," "Ibrahim," or "Ben Sande" bear silent testimony that the occupants are still mindful of the laws their forefathers set before them. On any day but the Sabbath these alleys composing the "Sûk es-Sâigh" are almost impassable. Women will sit for hours on the "mastaba," or door-step, watching their ornaments being made, or cheapening some necklace they contemplate purchasing. The patience of the merchant seems inexhaustible. I have seen the whole contents of his shop turned over without a single article being bought, and yet he would dismiss his visitor with the same blessing that a Christian dealer might only reserve for a solid customer. His coloured silk robes contrast curiously with the black garb of his female client. He knows nothing of her; the black veil that hides her face, with the exception of a pair of beautiful eyes, so disguises her that he would not recognise her again. She may come and sell her jewels here in public, and no one will be a bit the wiser as to who it is who has to realise. Were a man to dispose of his plate, the whole bazaar would soon know who he was, and be discussing the losses that compelled him to part with his valuables; for the Cairene is extremely inquisitive in everything relating to money. It cannot be said that the "Yashmak," with that curious brass cylinder fixed between the wearer's eyes to keep the veil in place, is becoming; its folds are tantalising, for should her nose, mouth and chin be as fine as her eyes, she must be a beautiful woman. Modesty compels her to hide her well-shaped figure in the long black shawl, but she enshrouds it with such art that its beauty gains rather than loses by the partial concealment. Contrary to her European sister, who adorns herself most lavishly when about to appear in public, *her* coloured garments, and the necklet she hopes to buy, will rejoice the eye of no man save her lord's, and will only be seen by her lady friends in the shelter of the "harem." This tantalising veil, which may hide so much beauty in her case, is a saving grace in many others. Compare her with the woman who is trying on an earring a few shops further on; here the "Yashmak" has been discarded, and her face proclaims her shame; her eyes would be beautiful had she not disfigured them with "Kohl," but her painted cheeks and coarse mouth decide one that, in her case, the veil would be very becoming—and the black shawl too, for her magenta dress with violet spots might well be blotted out of the picture.

As one advances further into this bazaar the air gets closer, and at every turning one looks ahead, hoping to see the main road again. Some "fellah" women, blocking the way, here thrust themselves into "Mousa's" cupboard of a shop, to let the "Sawarhine" pass. Slowly you move on, until at last you reach the Nahâssîn, and breathe freely once more.

Almost opposite to you now is the entrance to the Khân Khalîl, known also as the Turkish Bazaar. Built in 1300 by the Mameluke Sultan, El Ashraf Khalîl, it has ever since been the commercial centre of the old town, though its importance is doubtless very much less now that large shops and stores have sprung up in the new quarters of Cairo ; shops where a more or less fixed price saves the long and wearisome bargaining which a purchase in the native quarter entails. It is still, however, one of the liveliest and most picturesque places in the town. To the right you pass some large carpet stores, which you are politely asked to enter ; on your left silk merchants offer "Cufiyeh" for your inspection. These are silk shawls usually worn by Syrians instead of the turban. If you look like a possible purchaser, a Cingalee will press you to walk into his shop, and whisper that his goods are only half the price of his Moslem neighbour's. You pass on, and find yourself at the entrance of a slipper bazaar, where you look down an avenue of red and yellow slippers ; stacked on counters, hanging in festoons from the awnings, and in clusters round the doorways—everywhere slippers ! Red is the prevailing colour, for that is the hue the Cairene prefers for his foot-wear. The yellow ones are chiefly brought from Tunis or Morocco, and sold to the country folk. Rolls of red leather are stacked up in the little shops, where men are busy cutting, stitching and sewing slippers, and snips of red are strewn about the floors. No sooner is a stranger seen looking this way than a tout will thrust a pair of slippers under his nose :—" Only two shilling ! " " Come, see my shop." " Very cheap ! " You may vainly assure this bore that your portmanteau is stuffed with slippers ; that you have supplied all your friends and relations with slippers, and that you have come to loathe the sight of a red slipper. " Red slipper not good," answers the bore, " see my Tunis slippers " ; then, while he hurries off to get a yellow pair, you may slip into the carpet bazaar, as a means of escape. The carpet merchant has had his eye on you all the time ; others have tried this mode of escape. A handsome rug is deftly unrolled before you, while another thrown behind you cuts off your retreat. " Don't care for red carpets," you say in desperation ; and the moment he has turned his back to fetch a green one, you clear the prostrate rug and make for the outlet in front of you. You are in the main alley of the Khan once more, and at a safe distance from the red slippers, but the Cingalee, who can give the Arab points, has out-generalled you. He has a number of " Kuffiyeh " thrown over one shoulder, and while congratulating you that " Hussein," his neighbour, had not been able to foist his shoddy goods on you, he unfolds the shawl which he feels convinced will supply a long felt want. Your words, thrown out at random, about hating red slippers and not caring for red rugs, have not been lost on him. "No cheap German dyes here!" he whispers in pidjin English, and points to a rather prettily striped shawl he has thrown over his arm. He sees in an instant that the combination of colours has taken your fancy, though you may flatter yourself that you have not moved a muscle of your face. You ask the price, in spite of all your resolutions to buy nothing until you know more of the place. "Only six shilleen," articulates the Cingalee, confidentially, looking anxiously about to see that no other merchant has heard him underselling them in such a barefaced manner. He takes care not to notice your disapproval, but whispers why he is parting with this lovely garment so much below cost price. One good turn deserves another, and he feels sure that you will mention his name and give his card to all your friends at the hotel; then in slow and measured words, "*Kom widout de Dragoman!*" Politeness has so far failed to wipe this limpet off, and you decide upon a course of rudeness. This he receives with such grateful smiles that you begin to think he likes it. As a last resource you offer him a third of the price he asked, hoping that so dire an insult

will have some effect upon him ; but the beggar calmly wraps his shawl up in a piece of paper, hands it to you, and offers you a second at the same price. He leaves you standing there, one hand full of his cards, the parcel in the other, wondering why he did not try splitting the difference before so abruptly accepting your price. But the reason was soon evident ; a party of tourists, whose movements he had never lost sight of for one moment, had now entered the carpet bazaar at the entrance from which you had escaped, and would in due course emerge from the entrance opposite his stall. No time was to be lost splitting shillings where there was a possibility of splitting pounds. He had divined your hotel, and that of the new party, and gauged your spending powers in consequence. This kind of thing somewhat destroys the pleasure of a stroll through this otherwise delightful Khân.

One of the most enchanting spots is where the brass-workers ply their trade and expose their goods for sale. The Saracenic gateway with its stalactite vaulting and the quaint serpentine ornamentation is very beautiful. The original colouring has in most places disappeared, but what remains harmonises in a charming manner with the brown and pale gold of the stonework. It would be hard to conceive a finer setting for the brass lamps, bowls and dishes displayed upon the stalls on each side of the entrance. Lamps hang from every stall in the alley which leads to this gateway, and the one that crosses it at right angles. What a picture ! But where is one to sit to attempt to paint it ? My faithful Mohammed is a man of tact, but could all his ingenuity ever make this a possible task ? It seemed impossible to obtain a sketch of it without sitting in the middle of the lane, but the traffic is so great that an attempt from that point of vantage had to be given up as hopeless. Arrangements had to be made with a brass-worker to allow me to sit on his stall and to place some of his furniture between me and a too inquisitive crowd, who had soon formed up, three deep, to see what I was about. My knowledge of Arabic at that time was nil, so I remained in ignorance of the magic by which the faithful one was able to get all these concessions from the owner of the shop. The latter not only drove the small boys away, but served me with tea and cigarettes ; attentions which were rather embarrassing, as I knew I had begun a subject that meant a great many sittings, and I was not in a position to buy half his lamps to compensate him for the trouble I should give him. However, my work soon engrossed all my thoughts, and the friendly shopman ceased to exist for me. What a bothersome thing it was to paint! No sooner had I drawn some elaborate lamp, and was trying to get it into tone with its surroundings, than a tourist must have that particular one down for his inspection. I might be feeling rather pleased that a patch of sunlight was beginning to get its tonic value in my picture when down would come some awning, and that part of my subject would be blotted out. The noise of this awning descending would remind other shopmen that it was time for theirs to come down too, with the result that there would be very little of my subject left, and that little so altered in tone that no more painting was to be done that morning.

On my way home I asked the faithful one how he worked it with the shopman. "Well, I first told him that you were a nephew of Lord Cromer, and then hinted that it is just as well to make friends with those in power; besides this, I represented to him what an advertisement it will be for his shop when all the great people in Cairo see the picture." I retorted that I was not particularly fond of sailing under false colours. "Then, Sir, when you have finished I will tell him it was all lies," he complacently replied. The extraordinary thing is that in a place where lying is carried to such a fine art anyone could be found to believe these statements.

A good supply of cigarettes the next day aided me in further ingratiating myself with the vendor of lamps, and his numerous friends and relatives who came to his shop to have a peep at my work. The smoke also helped to keep the flies off. Each fresh acquaintance would try to assist me, either by cuffing a small boy who might try to get through the barrier of lamp-stands and chairs that Mohammed set up between me and the outside world, or by exhorting a neighbour not to move some of his goods till the "Hawaga" had finished painting them. I could have dispensed with much of this assistance; for if I attempted to blot in the colour of a man's robes, or draw the pose of another, these would-be assistants yelled out to my unconscious model to keep still. "He maketh thine ugly face to shine like a new brass bowl!" "Thou wilt be the admired of all the Nazarene ladies who behold his picture!" and such witticisms; which would generally cause my sitter to slip away, or, worse still, bring him round to see what I had made of him. The fame of my relationship to the great Proconsul had got winded about, for I was invited, right and left, to make use of the different shops as a temporary studio; and when once it was recognised that I came here to work and not to buy, touts ceased to pester me, and the Khân el Khalîl became one of my favourite sketching grounds.

Let us now resume our itinerary. A lane with one or two turnings takes us out of the Turkish

bazaar and into the " Muski," the Regent Street of " Masr el Kahira," which is the main thoroughfare, crossing the old town from East to West and connecting it with the new. European influence has crept up this street and it has become proportionately more common-place in appearance. We ascend it some couple of hundred yards and take the street to the right, where we are out of the draught of ugliness that blows up from the new town. The comparative quiet here is a relief, and is becoming to the precincts of the university which we are nearing. Appropriately enough, this is the street of the booksellers—" El Sharia el Halwagî " to give it its proper name. Copies of the Koran, old commentaries and text-books are ranged on the stalls, and the " Kutbi," or bookseller, is often a learned Sheykh himself who behaves with the dignity of his calling and does not try and foist his wares on you. We feel that we are indeed approaching Islam's great centre of learning.

CHAPTER IV

In the Streets of Cairo

The northern entrance of the Gâmiá el Azhar is soon visible. This is a little disappointing to the sketcher, who, having learnt that this University-Mosque was founded in the tenth century, is surprised to find such a new-looking building. Repeated additions and restorations make it hard to discover any traces of the original edifice which Gohar, the great vizier of the first Fatimid caliph, erected. One may regret a loss of picturesqueness due to the hand of the restorer in this and many other mosques, but had this work not been done, many a fine building would ere this have ceased to exist, or have remained but a shapeless mass of ruins. The increased value of the mosque endowments now permits of this work being carried on, and, happily, it is in the hands of so able an architect as Herz Bey, who has devoted a lifetime to the study of Saracenic architecture. Would that a man of equal knowledge had been found to

direct the restoration made in the time of Said Pasha! It is certainly now like a new patch in an old garment, for most of the houses that surround it, and all in that quarter, have a hoary look of antiquity, though none of these existed when the Azhar was first built.

To enter any moslem place of worship it is now necessary to procure tickets, which your guide or the hotel porter can obtain for you. The two piastres you pay for these correspond very much to the sixpence often necessary before being guided round an English cathedral. Time will not allow us to visit the interior this morning. Six minarets rise from this mosque, with apparently as little regard to plan as six flowering stems might rise from a clustre of lily bulbs, and two domes cover the resting place of the saintly founder. Unfortunately the buildings surrounding the university will not permit one to get far enough off to see more than one or two of these minarets at the same time. They are all varied in shape, and suggest different periods of construction. A late fifteenth century one is of especial beauty; the graduated transition from the square to the octagon and from the octagon to the circle; the clever concealment of the angles, with the stalactite pendentives which form the brackets supporting the galleries, deserve careful study. As each tier, defined by these galleries, rises from the mosque, the girth of the minaret becomes more slender, and the ornamentation is cleverly adapted to the increased height, the whole tending to lead the eye up to the egg-shaped finial that supports the emblem of their faith. The art of the builder has here reached its climax: its more pretentious neighbour of a later date looks awkward and top-heavy in comparison; it casts less beautiful shadows, and is inferior in the arrangement of the colour. The two domes built at greater intervals show this deterioration in an even more marked degree. The earlier one is, moreover, a true dome, and forms a dignified canopy for the tomb it covers, while the latter is only worthy to ornament a newspaper kiosk.

At a corner opposite the north side of the Azhar a double flight of stairs leads to a portal with very pretty stalactite vaulting. This is the entrance to a "medresseh," or college, which is often hard to distinguish from the congregational mosque. What is very surprising is to learn that it only dates back as far as 1774. The decadence in architectural style had set in long before that date, and yet there seems but little sign of this decadence here. Stanley Lane Poole tells us that it was built on the plan of an earlier mosque at Boulak, it is therefore probable that while copying the plan they copied the detail

also. This, with the surrounding stalls below, and a peep of the dome rising above the arabesque balustrade, silhouetted against the deep blue sky, forms a subject that few painters would pass without looking round for a suitable spot to set up an easel. Were I writing a guide book for artists, I would mark this with two stars.

Sharp round the corner a zig-zag lane soon takes you into "El Ashrafîyeh," the main street which is a continuation of El Nahâssîn, and you have returned to the full noise and bustle of the busy part of Cairo. Here are more huge mosques, touching and facing each other, domes and minarets breaking the perspective of the street, and forming an ever-varying skyline as you pass along. Once more the shouts from the camel-drivers, donkey-boys, and hawkers greet your ears. A blue-shirted cabman is trying to drive his load of tourists through this motley crowd. The dragoman sitting next to him on the box assists him in exhorting the foot-passengers to make way. "Oah ja gedda!" "Oah ishmaelak!" "Oah riglak!" "Iftah eynak ja am!" ("Look out, oh workman," "Look out to your left," "Take care of your feet," "Open thine eye, oh uncle!") they alternately cry out. The tourists look worn-out and dazed; so much has been crowded into one morning. One youth has just sufficient energy left to take a few flying shots with his Kodak ; but whether he records the camel, or only a passing sunshade, does not seem to disturb him very much. Facing you, on one side of the stairs of the mosque of Ghûrî, and almost hidden by the awnings of the adjoining booth, there is a little passage which leads into the scent bazaar. Here you are offered, for four or five shillings, a little phial of attar of roses containing four or five drops. This covered passage, with the usual cup-board-like shops and "mastaba," leads into a maze of narrow lanes, in each of which one particular trade is plied, or one class of goods sold. The spice bazaar is particularly interesting, and often more beautiful in colour than any other ; cinnamon, cloves, nutmegs and aloes heaped around the merchant harmonise deliciously with his silk robes, and the bags, baskets and matting that comprise the furniture of his shop. You can wander next through the Tunis and Algerian bazaars, others given up to shoemakers and to dealers in woollen goods from Arabia, and so work your way once more into the main street not far from the great mosque of El Muaiyad.

This imposing building was erected by the Circassian Mameluke Sultan, El Muaiyad, in 1416, to serve as a "medresseh" or college, many of which existed at that period : but as the students gradually flocked to the "azhar," these "medressa" were converted into congregational mosques. This one is also the mausoleum of its founder and his family. A great builder was "El Muaiyad," for, in spite of the troublous times in which he lived, six mosques, two colleges and a hospital—the "Maristan El Muaiyad"—are recorded as dating from his reign of ten years. Saracenic architecture had reached its highest point a century earlier. The magnificent bronze doors were originally those of the Sultan Hasan Mosque, to which we shall refer later on.

The chief interest, however, of this part of Cairo is not this mosque, but the old town gate which adjoins it, and which crosses the street we are now in. The Bâb ez-Zuwêleh took its name from a tribe of Berber auxiliaries who were quartered just outside. It is one of the three great gates in the wall that separated Kahira from the sites of the more ancient Fostât and Katâi, and was built by the Armenian vizier Bedr during the caliphate of El Mustansir in 1070. From that time until the Othmanly conquest of Egypt in 1517 it was associated with nearly every dramatic event that happened in Cairo. The massive square bastions, the round arch of the gate, and the vaulting of the passage are more Byzantine than Saracenic in character. Its towers were shortened to receive the twin minarets that El Muaiyad erected when he built his mosque, but otherwise it is little altered. Stanley Lane Poole, in his fascinating "Story of Cairo," tells us of many a tragic scene that this grim gate has witnessed. He relates how, in 1154, Nasr, the murderer of the "Fauceant" caliph El-Zâhir, was delivered up by the Templars of Palestine, for a blood money of £30,000, to the women of the palace, who tortured him and sent him through the streets of Cairo, maimed and blinded, to be crucified alive at the Bâb ez-Zuwêleh. Ten years later, the vizier Dargham was ignominiously slain here. He was a brave paladin who fought the Crusaders at Gaza, but lost his cause by laying impious hands on the mosque endowments to pay his troops. Deserted by his followers, whose idol he had lately been, he was pursued by an infuriated mob through this gateway, his head was hacked off, and his body thrown into the ditch to be worried by the pariah dogs. When the orthodox and famous Saladin succeeded the last of the puppet caliphs, he rigorously put down a rising of the black troops who still adhered to the Shîa heresy ; and a terrible slaughter, which lasted two days, took place outside the Zuwêleh Gate. When the Mongol envoys came to Cairo with insulting demands of submission, the Mameluke Kutuz cut off their heads and exposed them to the populace here. Passing through the passage, you face a house at the corner of the street which is more or less the continuation of the one

you have left. Its distinguishing feature is a large iron grating and the column which is built into the corner. This column, which appears to have been put there as an ornamental chamfer, was for years the place of execution ; malefactors being strangled against the shaft. Small wonder that this gate is looked upon by Cairenes as a haunted spot! With them it goes more often by the name of Bâb el-Mitwelli. On the door on your left as you pass out you will notice coloured bits of rags covering a large part of it, you may also see teeth hanging by a string from nails, as well as other unpleasing objects.

Should you be sketching here long, you will see people pry mysteriously behind this door, and then proceed to drive a nail into it. I was a good deal exercised in my mind when first I worked there, till the faithful Mohammed enlightened me to a certain extent. It appeared that a certain "Kutb el-Mitwelli," a saint of exceeding sanctity, is believed to frequent the niche behind this door ; but as he has the power of rendering himself invisible, it is hard to get ocular proof of his presence ; he can also, I was told, change his place in an instant ; therefore when you think you have caught him in his niche, he may have transported himself unseen to the top of the Kaaba at Mekka. He possesses great curative powers, for it is well proved that if a tooth aches very much, and you pull it out and fasten it to the door, it will very soon cease to give you pain ! Mothers will bring sore-eyed children and press their faces against the woodwork ; and it is as well for the unbeliever not to attempt a similar cure, for he might get a worse disease than the one he was seeking to relieve. A queer-looking saint occasionally squats in front of this door, who is an object of great veneration. No mediæval artist has ever clad a Lazarus in such a patchwork of rags. His wild look, and the spear he clutches, prevents even the " Giour " from treating him with disrespect. What the connection of this saint and the mysterious " el-Mitwelli " is I have never been able to fathom, but I shall try again when next I set up my easel within reach of his spear.

The accompanying illustration is from a drawing I made of the twin minarets of El Muaiyad, which rise so gracefully from the blood-stained Bâb ez-Zuwêleh. The intervening houses hide the gateway that has taxed the powers of many brother brushes to get an adequate presentment of. The space around it is too confined to get it within the focus of a picture ; and perhaps it is just as well that the shambles from which these lovely minarets spring should be hidden, even as the garden soil hides the filth lying at the roots of two beautiful lilies.

These towers are much the same in character as the one we particularly noticed on the Azhar. The Circassian Sultans of the fifteenth century delighted in this elaborate ornamentation ; and their work has not the simplicity nor the grandeur of that of the fourteenth century, as we shall see when we compare it with the earlier work of the Sultan Hasan. In most cases the narrowness of the streets prevents one from seeing the mosques as a whole, but the simpler character of the houses which partially hide them suggest in a picture those broad spaces that the fourteenth century architects understood so well the value of.

It is curious that El Mahmûdi Muaiyad should have chosen the flanking towers of the Zuwêleh as a base for the minarets which belong to his adjoining mosque and mortuary. For some time he lay, a prisoner of his unruly subjects, in this very gate. He was a pious Moslem of the now orthodox faith that Saladin, before him, had purged of the Shîa heresy ; and we are also told that he was a man of learning, a poet, orator, and musician ; very simple in his mode of living and in his dress ; robing himself in common white wool as a sign of mourning for the pestilence that ravaged his land. He was intolerant, nevertheless, of those of another faith, and the fine monuments he erected were principally paid for from the exactions he levied on the Christians and the Jews. He enforced the sumptuary laws, which for a long time had been in abeyance; the Copts being obliged to wear blue cloaks and black turbans, while the cloak of the Jew had to be yellow and his turban black as that of the Christian. To distinguish them still more from the true believer, a heavy cross had to hang from the neck of one, and a black ball from that of the other. Though it is long since these laws have been enforced, I cannot recall ever having seen either a Christian or Jew in a white turban, which is the one most commonly worn by the Moslem.

We now follow the "Derb el Ahmar," the street on the left as you emerge from the gate, and take one more look at El Muaiyad's minarets, which are here seen dominating a group of mouldering old houses, whose creamy colour they carry up into the blue.

Here I have often seen an old man bending under the weight of a large pitcher of water slung across his back; the mouth of this vessel is closed with a rag stopper, but a metal spout rising from its shoulder projects above that of the man, who, by bending a little more, allows the water to trickle into a cup he holds in his hand. A passer by will often drain this cup and only reward him with a blessing, and this seems to satisfy the old man, for again he will bend forward to refill it repeating the doleful song that first made me notice him. My guide also slackening his thirst, and not parting with a "fadda" in return, caused me to chaff him about getting a drink on the cheap, and I got him to repeat to me the burthen of the old man's song. It was as nearly as possible the opening verse of Isaiah lv., for it might be translated as follows: "Ho, every one that thirsteth, come ye to this water, and he that hath no money, come ye and drink, without money and without price!" This custom probably dates back to days long before Mohammed, and possibly to the days of Isaiah himself. Now stand-pipes have been erected in most parts of the city, and a good supply of water laid on, this pretty custom may fall into disuse: but let us hope that the charitable people who supported these old water carriers may find some fresh outlet for their benefactions!

You pass the little mosque of Ishmâs-el-Ishâki at the fork of two streets, and a charming sebil on your right with some pretty tiles and a richly-coloured ceiling; another mosque on your left, and you come to the beautiful one of El-Merdani. This mosque was in a deplorable state of ruin when I first saw it, and though most artists fight shy of newly-restored buildings, I rejoice that the commission for the preservation of Arab monuments have taken it in hand. The restorations have been carried out by Herz Bey; and the work has been so satisfactorily done that one is able here fully to appreciate the state of perfection Sarcenic art had reached during the first half of the fourteenth century. A good deal of the original wood carving has found its way into museums—South Kensington, amongst others, has some good examples.

A narrow little street which passes one side of the Merdani leads into a larger street of that name. Houses suggesting a decaying aristocracy are to the right and left of you. One with a handsome doorway and a few bay windows, and with the meshrebiya broken or patched with bits of packing-cases, premises that the owner has either fallen on bad times, or on times sufficiently good to enable him to build a new house in the Ismailîyeh quarter, leaving the rats and some pensioned-off old eunuch in quiet possession of this one. I have often found interesting courtyards in similar houses, but it is difficult to get a sight of them. The massive door is often open, but the passage leading to the interior court after a few yards generally takes a sharp turn, which effectually shuts out the view from the outside world.

My faithful guide was at his best here. I had but

W. Tyndale

to look wistfully at one of these mysterious portals and, like the Kodak people, he "would do the rest." Should the house be in a deserted "cul de sac," and should there be no one from whom he could get any information as to the occupants, he would boldly dive in. If he returned quickly the chances were that there was nothing interesting to see or to paint, for he had a good idea of what I was in search of; but sometimes he would find the place quite deserted, or the caretaker fast asleep, when he would steal out and beckon to me to step in and have a peep. Should there be anything as good as in the accompanying illustration, I would leave it to him to arrange matters as well as he could. Sometimes the matter could be settled at once, the prospect of a shilling or two thoroughly awakening the custodian; at other times, as in this instance, it would be necessary to find the owner, and it might be a day or two before I could start a drawing. If the house was an important one, the harem was often the difficulty, especially if the entrance to the ladies' department chanced to be the doorway which I desired to paint. In this particular case I was good-naturedly told by the owner that, during the heat of the day, none of his women-folk would want to stir out, so that I was welcome to paint until the ladies were ready to "smell the air," as he expressed it. My painting his eunuch fast asleep at the doorway of his harem seemed to amuse the proprietor vastly; especially when the eunuch complained that he was in too hot a corner, and I had to get Mohammed to hold a parasol, in order that the sun's rays might not injure the blackie's complexion.

The ladies had evidently been watching these proceedings through the meshrebiya; for when the eunuch had been roasted long enough to allow me to complete his picture, some whispering and giggling ended in his asking to be allowed to take my drawing inside, to show it to the "Sittât." My picture—which is not meant to be a humorous one—seemed to strike the "Sittât" as such, for peals of laughter now proceeded from the other side of the curtain. The eunuch presently returned with my drawing, looking very crestfallen, and he wept as he enlarged on all the indignities I had subjected him to: but a little more "baksheesh," and, as someone remarks in the Pilgrim's Progress, "I saw him no more."

This street of El-Merdani is a short one and soon ends in the "Sûk el-Sellâha,"—the armourers' market. The stillness of the former street is enlivened here by the tap, tap, of the gunmakers and the sound of the bellows. Wild-looking Bedouin or Syrian Arabs are having the flint locks of their long guns repaired; old blunderbusses, spears, and a few modern fowling-pieces hang about the shops, and nondescript bits of iron and brass strew the floors ; but it is a poor show these gunsmiths make now, compared with bygone days, when this Suk was the arms factory of the sultans. The lower story is often all that is left of some former armourer's abode. A partially ruined mosque, with a pretty fluted pattern on the dome, and a minaret which is a peril to the "muezzin" every time he ascends it to call these smiths to prayer, complete this picture of dilapidation.

The top of the Sûk joins the avenue Mohammed Ali, and sight-seeing is over for this morning. A tramway coming down from the citadel is the quickest way of getting over the mile of uninteresting road that leads to the European quarter of Cairo.

CHAPTER V

OLD CAIRO

SHOULD the reader care to follow me once more through some of the old quarters of the town, we can again take this tramway at the Ezbekîyeh Gardens, and alight about half-way up the Sharia Mohammed Ali, near the "Bâb el-Khalk." This wide avenue was ruthlessly run through the old city by Egypt's first Khedive, after whom it is named. Many interesting buildings were swept away to make this roadway up to the citadel. Howls of indignation arose from all pious Moslems in Egypt when they heard that the sacred shrines, mosques, and other structures connected with their faith were being ruthlessly torn down; but Ali was all powerful, and not the man to allow the religious scruples of his people to stand in his way, as he had shown them upon a former occasion, when he seized on the Wakfs, or religious endowments, and diverted them to secular uses. He doubtless did much for his newly acquired country, but it is ever

Walter Tyndale

to be regretted that he was such a Philistine in matters of taste.

The large new building on your left, *en style Arabe*, is the museum of Arabian art. A good number of its contents are spoils from the wreck that Mohammed Ali made of many parts of the city; and many a fine piece of mosque furniture is also there which one would gladly see restored to the original buildings, that are still extant, and from which they have been taken. It is a fine collection, and anyone interested in Arab wood and metal work can study it here to his heart's content.

We can here hire donkeys, if the weather is too hot for a long walk, and go along the Derb el-Gamâmîz, a long street of which the houses on the west side back upon the now filled-in canal, El-Khalig; it is a main thoroughfare that, under various names, crosses the city from north to south, keeping parallel with the canal the whole way. It is quieter than the main streets near the Khan el Khalîl, as it is some distance from the chief bazaars. In the early morning you may here meet camels laden with foodstuffs, and cattle and sheep driven in from the country on their way to the various markets. It is a pretty sight to see these camels in the summer, with their loads of gourds and melons in coarse, open network panniers, suspended from their backs. The driver sometimes retails these as he goes along, carrying a cut water-melon in his hand. He stops at every fruit-stall on the chance of doing a more wholesale deal; and this is a long process, often keeping the camel standing long enough to allow of a careful drawing being made. These fruit-stalls, which are rigged up in any odd corner, or the more permanent shops, filled with apples, oranges, and lemons, and backed by piles of melons, make a delightful patch of colour in most of the streets. The salesman from an inherited instinct seems to feel the right colour for the paper and tinsel with which he surrounds his goods, and, as the season advances, tall bundles of sugar-cane lean against the wall, or fill any awkward angle, with their long, greyish-green leaves.

When it is one's fate to remain in Cairo during the heat of the summer, or early autumn, one is to a certain extent compensated by the increased beauty of the streets. The shapes and shadows of the awnings which are slung across the roads, or propped up with poles over the shops and stalls, add enormously to the picturesqueness. These large canvases and bits of matting admit sufficient light through them to impart a warm glow without casting too black a shadow. The people, also, are much more picturesque in their summer garments; for the ugly bits of European clothing often worn over their "gelabieh," are only seen during the comparatively cold weather. Nor are the tourists, there, whose dress harmonises so badly with eastern surroundings. Children play about half-naked, and their elders move in a manner more becoming to the dignity of an oriental. So much more goes on in the streets here than in more northern countries; the goods for sale are displayed on the pavement, and shops, as Europeans know them, are not seen.

A little way down the Derb el-Gamâmîz, through a large doorway, up some steps, you get a peep into a Dervish monastery. The large paved courtyard, beautified by trees and a pretty tiled fountain, looks inviting from a hot and dusty street. Some sycamore trees are also in the roadway near here, justifying the name "gamâmîz," opposite these is the gate of the Viceregal Library. To students of oriental languages this library is all important, and to those more interested in the art of the country than in its literature it is well worth a visit, were it but to see the illuminated copies of the Koran which it contains. Every facility is here given to European students, and this is not always the case in a Moslem library, which is usually almost entirely devoted to works connected with the religion of Mahommed.

The Ministry of Education is next door. Of

all the tasks entailed by the British occupation of Egypt, there is none more difficult, nor one requiring more tact and discretion, than that of directing the course of study to be pursued by the young Moslem. As in the Azhar university at present, so in past days the teaching in all schools consisted almost entirely in expounding passages of the Koran. Pages of this book did the scholars have to commit to memory while their reasoning faculties were hardly exercised at all. Now, Oxford and Cambridge men teach them mathematics, history, and geography, and generally prepare them to hold their own, in later life, under the changed conditions of their country. All this is excellent, but unfortunately it does not stop there. An idea is current that Europeanisation must go hand in hand with progress; therefore, instead of developing their own civilisation, an alien one is gradually being thrust upon them. To take but one instance,—no pupil is allowed to attend the Khedival schools in the becoming dress of his forefathers, but must wear coat and trousers, and dress generally like the "Firangi," except for the absurd red tarbouch. Now what moral or civilising effect can a pair of trousers have? Once accustomed to these ugly garments they will wear them all their lives. Their beautiful houses, so admirably planned to suit a hot climate, are rapidly

disappearing ; it is hard that their picturesque dress should not be left to them.

We will walk a little further down this street till we reach a pretty "sebîl" on our left ; then, turning sharply round this fountain, we face the entrance to one of these Khedival schools. The illustration is from a drawing I did some ten years ago, before these sumptuary laws came into force. The youngsters as they hurry out of the school now make a very different picture. Suits, cheaply run together in some sweater's den in Europe, have replaced the "gelabieh" and flowing "tôb." The change seems to have affected their manners as well as their appearance, for their bearing is now no more dignified than their clothes. Their former robes were easier to wash than tweed suits are ; thus from a sanitary point of view there is a distinct loss, and I have heard the poorer natives complain of the extra expense that this new outfit entails. The argument that they are not compelled to send their children to these schools is not worth answering.

Let us now skirt round this building and take a lane in a southerly direction. High walls here enclose the gardens of some pasha's house. We follow these, and pass one or two mosques of more or less importance, but each with some character peculiar to itself. We come presently to the house of the Sheykh Sadaat, but some fine meshrebiya bay windows are all the outside world can see of the beauty of this grand old house. It was my good fortune to have been introduced to the late Sheykh by a mutual friend, therefore I was allowed to paint there as much as I pleased. No house more recalls to my mind the pictures of Lewis. An enormous willow grows in the courtyard, its leaves brush against the beautiful lattice-work of the windows, and under its shade a fountain plays. The private mosque of the Sheykh is at one corner of this court and the entrance of the large reception-room at the other, while in a room between the two the old man generally received his guests, whom he would invite to sit on the raised cushioned floor upon which he reclined.

When I first visited him, the sight of this old man in his yellow silk robes and enormous turban, sitting cross-legged on a Persian rug, with a yellow silk cushion to ease his back, and the smoke curling from his "chibouk" making the little touch of cool colour in a harmony of pale gold—the whole seemed to suggest a very clever "tableau vivant" after some picture of Benjamin Constant's. At that time I could not speak or understand a word of Arabic, and it was moreover my first introduction to an oriental grandee. I could not *say* the wrong thing, as my friend, Choucri Tabet, who introduced me, would be sure to interpret any remarks of mine in the way most pleasing to our host ; but I was nervous about *doing* the wrong thing, and felt rather at a disadvantage in my very ordinary attire. This slight awkwardness, however, was only of short duration. Coffee and cigarettes were handed round by a blackamoor, almost before the first greetings were concluded, and my friend and host were soon engaged in a lively conversation. Some joke would make the old gentleman hold his sides with laughter, and then, fearing lest I might feel a bit out of it, he would insist on my friend's interpreting it to me ; and when he was sure that I fully appreciated the point he would laugh again till the tears rolled down his cheeks. His appearance and his beautiful surroundings made such an impression on me as quite to obliterate from my memory what the subject of the joke was. It was a charming place to be allowed to paint and I hope that, should opportunity permit, the dear old Sheykh's successors may prove equally kind, and accord me the same privilege.

These houses have been slowly evolved by the necessities of the climate and the social and religious laws of the people. To make life bearable during the many months of hot weather, and to preserve the privacy of the weaker sex, have ever been the first considerations of the Saracenic builder. The open arcaded hall, facing north and overlooking a spacious courtyard, is only suitable in a southern climate. The separate entrance to the harem, which has its rooms either overlooking a garden or a court of its own, and the careful masking of the windows that may have to face the street, are considerations that need trouble no northern architect. These meshrebiya windows, which allow the outside world to be seen and yet hide the beholder, are also used in the men's part of the house to screen the rays of the sun while admitting a free circulation of air. Koranic law, even if it does not actually prohibit, has never encouraged the presentment of natural objects as a basis of decoration ; yet its followers have shown how possible it is to ornament their buildings with great beauty despite this drawback. The narrowness of the streets permits a visit to a neighbour or attendance at a mosque without having to step out of the shade, while the large courtyards and gardens give the required air-spaces. As the richer folk are gradually leaving these quarters to live in the newer town, the sanitary arrangements are shockingly neglected, and ever tend to increase this exodus. Indeed, properly to drain old Cairo may possibly

W. Tyndale

be the only means of saving it from complete ruin.

We now skirt the wall of the Sadaat's garden, and after one or two turns we pass the mosque of Hasan Pasha. Though this was built some three centuries after Arab architecture had reached its highest perfection, it is still a very artistic structure. Its style is not equal to the great work of the fourteenth and fifteenth centuries, but fortunately the decline of architecture was as slow a process as its rise had been. To give a very felicitous quotation from Stanley Lane Poole's "Story of Cairo,"—"Everything in the East changes by almost imperceptible degrees, and the mills of God in Egypt grind with the tedious slowness of the creaking sakujas of the country."

The surroundings of this mosque help its pictorial value considerably. For one thing, space allows of its being seen from a sufficient distance to take in the whole of the exterior, with the picturesque little arcaded school above the sebîl, and a tree which seems to have grown there for the sole purpose of improving the composition. It is all in a warm, rich key of colour. The alternating courses of red and buff-coloured stone which may have looked crude when Hasan Pasha was laid to rest here are now beautifully blended together; time has also dealt kindly with the rather over-elaborate detail. It is still sharply defined above, where the afternoon sun emphasises the drawing, but it is worn away at the base, and at the entrance by the countless worshippers who have crossed its threshold. It looks in sound repair, so let us hope that no restorations may be needed here for some time; for however well they may be done they cannot fail to rob it of much of its charm and poetry.

In Cairo it is not necessary to go back to a remote period to find beautiful architecture, for the dwelling-houses were built on the old lines right up to the end of the eighteenth century, and the beautiful example we have referred to, the Sadaat's house, is not two hundred years old. The periods are difficult to mark in Egypt, for there was never here the violent change in style which Europe witnessed during the Renaissance. Things went on much the same until Mohammed Ali's accession in 1805, and since that time Arab architecture has not changed, but has ceased to exist. I doubt whether a native Cairene architect, with any knowledge of the building art of his forefathers, could now be found. The few houses built in the so-called "style Arabe" are designed by Europeans, and the restoration of the monuments is now in the hands of Christians. Let us hope that some day the Egyptian may himself awaken to the fact that the architecture of his forbears is more beautiful and better suited to his climate and surroundings than that of the nondescript erections which are now run up in the modern quarters of his city, and that a new Cairo, built upon the lines of the old city, may yet arise, to delight all lovers of the suitable and the picturesque.

CHAPTER VI

The Mosque of Ibn Tulûn

Continuing our walk in a southerly direction along what might be called the "Faubourg St. Germain" of the old town, we pass the mosque of Ezbek el-Yusefi and wander on through some deserted looking streets until we reach the "Sharia" Tulûn. The houses about here appear more dilapidated than ever, but here and there a fine display of meshrebiya bay windows and a handsome doorway remind us that we are still in what was once the aristocratic part of the city. A sharp turning takes you up a narrow lane and you are at the entrance gate of the mosque of Ibn Tulûn. Little of the exterior is visible from here as partly ruined houses butt against the outside walls. We mount a flight of stairs, pass under a high archway, and enter the outer court which extends round three sides of this huge enclosure. We then ascend some more steps on our left, pass through one of the cloisters of the Liwan, and enter the

inner court. The size and desolation of this mosque is what strikes one most; the silence also is awe-inspiring; no sound from the outside world penetrates to this enclosure, and the dust of ages deadens the sound of our footsteps.

The stories we are told concerning this mosque seem less legendary as the enchantment of the place takes hold of us. The plateau on which we stand is on a part of the hill of Yeshkur which has had a hallowed reputation from time immemorial. We are told that here Moses communed with Jehovah, that prayers offered up here are more likely to be answered than those from any other place, and we are not far from the Kalat-el-Kebsh (the castle of the ram) where Abraham is believed to have made his burnt offering, very much to the relief of his little son Isaac.

The story of how the money was obtained to build this great structure also savours of the miraculous. Ahmed Ibn Tulûn, while wandering over the Mokattam hills found a great treasure concealed in a cave called "Pharaoh's oven." This providential find he vowed he would dedicate to Allah and build a mosque large enough to hold the whole population of his capital. The site seemed clearly indicated, no other than this hallowed spot at the edge of, and dominating, his new faubourg El-Kataî, and far from the mosque of Amr in the centre of Fostât, but close to his palace and the houses of his nobles.

Plans were drawn out by his greatest architects; but a difficulty here arose. The great Emir was a man of culture and a scholar, and would not sanction the destroyal of the temples to furnish him with the columns, 600 of which were required. His tolerance also forbade his demolishing the Christian churches for that purpose. A Coptic architect who was at the time a prisoner in El-Kataî submitted a plan to solve the difficulty. He proposed to substitute for the columns piers built of burnt brick, reserving but two pillars of coloured marble to stand on each side of the "Kibla." The grandeur and originality of the design was appreciated by Ibn Tulûn, and the Coptic prisoner was entrusted with the carrying out of his plans. This fine mosque, worthy of the sacred site it covers, was begun in 876 and completed in two years. It has done more than any other great work of its founder to keep the name of Ibn Tulûn fresh in the memories of his countrymen.

The Liwan, or cloister, at the south-eastern side, where the "Kibla," the niche that points in the direction of Mekka, stands, is formed of five rows of arches, one of which has now disappeared, while a double row runs round the other three sides of the square. The general plan is that of most mosques of from the ninth to the twelfth century ; but a striking feature is the presence of the pointed arch at so early a date. There is a slight inward curve where it springs from the pier, but not sufficient to remind one of the Moorish horseshoe arch. At the corners of the piers a half column is let in and serves as a chamfer. A smaller arch, of similar proportions, pierces the spaces between the larger ones, which lightens the appearance and also lessens the weight the piers have to carry. A running pattern, round both arch and the tops of the piers, relieves the otherwise extreme severity of the design. This ornamentation was all worked with a tool in the plaster while this was still moist, and has a life about it that no casting or stencilling can give. The magnificent wooden pulpit is, alas ! but a skeleton of what it was. The place was for so long uncared for, that most of the ornament within reach has been stolen, either to sell to the collector of curios or even for use as firewood. The Kibla, surrounded with a double arch, supported on two pairs of marble columns, is richly embellished with mosaics and precious stones. Its proportions are very fine, and it is a gem of colour, while the old Kufic lettering of the texts above add greatly to the character of the place, and are most decorative.

One gets charming perspective views while moving along under the shadow of this liwan and looking crosswise through these arcades into the patch of sunlight in the open court. A curious corkscrew shaped tower, which can hardly be called a minaret, rises out of the walls at the north-east corner. This is well worth ascending, for you will obtain a grand view of Cairo from its summit. Nearly the whole of the old quarters of the city are spread out to the north of you. Innumerable domes and minarets rise everywhere from this mass of houses ; some singly, while others, where they are relieved one against the rest, appear to be in clusters. Were Ibn Tulûn permitted in spirit to see this sight, he would find it hard to realise that he was standing on the tower he built. In his day, nothing of what we now behold existed. Save a few Arab tents, not a habitation was here ; there was then only marshy land, submerged during the high Nile, to your left, and a sandy waste to the right. Far away to the west the Emir would still recognise the Pyramids, as unchangeable as the Mokattam hills to the east ; but this would be all which could recall the country that he had ruled a thousand years ago. El Kaluro was non-existent then. To the south he would vainly seek his royal faubourg of " El-Katâi," amidst the rather squalid houses now standing ; " El-Askar" is no more, and only the hill of Babylon now attests the spot where Amr built the " Town of the Tent," or Fostât.

Perhaps the most impressive sight to us now is this great desolate mosque immediately beneath us. The veneration the site was held in must have attracted thousands of worshippers; the various tribes that composed the Emir's army, who were quartered in the cantonments just outside, will have filled this great court when some noted Sheykh preached here to inflame their enthusiasm before starting on their campaigns. Saladin will here have offered up thanks to Allah after worsting the Crusaders, and have prayed that the Crescent might finally triumph over the Cross. But the belief that prayers are more likely to be answered in this sacred spot than in any other fails to draw worshippers here now. That it might be haunted with "Affrits" might easily suggest itself to the imaginative oriental, and he might feel safer in repairing to a less dilapidated place of worship, and one less frequented by these unpleasant beings. The artist who fights shy of an admiring crowd may work here in safety, and may thank the lurking "Affrit" for so effectually keeping off the small boys.

We now follow the "Sharia Tulûn" for about half a mile, when we come in sight of the mosque of Mohammed Ali which crowns the citadel. There is always something to interest one while strolling along any of these streets, for every important event in the life of the Cairene has some manifestation in the streets. Those red flags, hung across the mysterious little alley which we look down, betoken either a marriage or a birth. The noise of hautbois and drums in the distance suggests the latter. Presently a procession headed by musicians turns into the main street and approaches this alley; the boy carrying the barber's sign tells you that a circumcision is also being celebrated, for the humbler folk will often combine several family events to lessen the expense. Two or three camels, caparisoned in gorgeous cloths of red and gold, with tassels swinging from their necks, carry each a pair of kettle-drums, which the driver, sitting cross-legged on the hump, is vigorously belabouring. Several carriages follow, crammed with little boys dressed in the gayest colours; these are the companions of the one or two little chaps who have made their first acquaintance with the barber, who, as in former times in England, combines surgery with the tonsorial art.

A closed carriage forms the rear, and lattice sashes, or a close drawn curtain, carefully conceal the bride. Sometimes she is carried to her new home in a little swing between two camels, fore and aft. When funds allow, another set of musicians follow this cortege; but more often the female relatives and friends bring up the rear, uttering a shrill noise betokening joy, called "el gaharit." The poor bride has a long day of it, for, previous to the wedding, a similar procession follows her to the baths, and this is called "Zeffet el Hamman." The furniture of her new house is also paraded through the streets; those curious, long, two-wheeled donkey-carts being used for the purpose.

The upper classes generally adopt the Turkish marriage customs, and the ceremonial and festivities are more confined to the house, but in neither case does the bridegroom see the features of his bride until the wedding has taken place.

My wife and one of my sons were invited to attend the marriage festivities at the house of a pasha where all was conducted "à la Turque." The day had been spent by the principals in going through the more serious formalities, and most of the wedding guests only arrived at eight or nine in the evening. My wife and my son,—who was still too young to be objected to on the score of sex,—were conducted into the harem, while I had to join the male portion of the family, and their numerous friends, in the courtyard. Gaily coloured hangings and Chinese lanterns brightened the scene, coffee and cigarettes were continually handed round, also sherbet and other non-intoxicating drinks, and on a large daïs some musicians were playing an accompaniment to the singing of the local Sims

Reeves. The expression of approval of the audience, which grew more marked as the song proceeded, was the only evidence I had that we were listening to an exceptionally fine vocalist. Personally, I could not greatly appreciate it, and I was relieved when a servant later on informed me that the "Sitt" (my wife) was ready to drive back to the hotel. Greater familiarity with Arab music has taught me to appreciate it more, but to feel the raptures that my fellow guests did is only given to those who are born to it!

I was curious to know what had taken place in the harem. The gathering of ladies there, I was told, very much resembled a similar one in Europe. The black silk shawl which envelops their smart clothes when they are in the outer world, was not necessary here, nor the yashmak that hides their features. As my wife knew no one, and the conversation was carried on almost entirely in Arabic, she confessed to feeling somewhat out of it. The event of the evening, however, compensated her, for, shortly before our departure, the bridegroom, with his brothers and some friends, left our company and proceeded to the entrance of the harem, where they knocked loudly at the door, and when this was opened, the young man about to be made happy bade adieu to his companions and entered. His veiled bride was there

Walter Tyndale

to meet him, and then, in the presence of her relations, the young man uncovered her face and gazed on her features for the first time. The lady guests then thought it discreet to retire, and carriages were ordered to draw up.

Arriving at the end of the street where we have been entertained by this marriage procession, we cross the Place Rumeleh, and ascend the slope leading to the citadel. Mohammed Ali chose a grand site for his mosque and tomb, and, considering the date of its construction—the middle of the last century—we may be thankful that its exterior is still so fine. We may regret that his architect did not seek his inspiration from some of the grand monuments which it overlooks, instead of copying a mosque in Constantinople, but we may be thankful that he did not go to Paris for his model! The Madeleine, well as it looks in the French capital, would have been as much out of place here as is that "imitation of a boulevard," the "Sharia Mohammed Ali," which leads to the mosque. Sightseers, though they may have but one day in which to do Cairo, are always conducted here; and the cost of the alabaster used in the interior, and that of the ballroom chandeliers suspended from the dome seems to interest a great many. Let us content ourselves in this instance with a glance at the exterior, and so turn to the view from the parapet at the south-west corner. It is, of course, much the same as that which kept us so long on the tower of Ibn Tulûn; but, seen from a fresh point of view, one can enjoy the changed grouping of the domes and minarets which rise from the pale, buff mass of houses beneath us. We can follow the course of the Nile from the far southern horizon till it loses itself in the Delta, formed during countless ages by its fertilising deposit. The strip of green on each side of its banks alternately widens or contracts, clearly marking the reach of the life-giving waters during the inundations. We again view the Pyramids, relieved against the hills of the Libyan desert, and we promise ourselves to return here some evening when the sun will beat down on us less strongly, and when we shall see it sink into the west.

The deserted mosque of Gamia Ibn Kâlâun is hidden behind its modern and more prosperous-looking neighbour. It was used until quite recently as a military storehouse, and previous to that it had served as a prison. The dome has fallen in, most of the coloured marble which adorned the interior has gone, yet enough remains to show that it was worthy of the great Mameluke Sultan who built it. El-Násir's palace formerly stood near it, but this, with its famed "Hall of Columns," had to make way for the mosque of Mohammed Ali.

On the south-east we come to Joseph's well, "Bir

Yûsuf." Tradition tells us that this is the pit into which Joseph was cast by his brethren, and though tradition is out in its topography by some 300 miles, this story is still firmly believed by many, and is solemnly repeated by some of the dragomans. Though having no connection with the Joseph of scripture, it is interesting to learn that it takes its name from "Salâhedden Y-ûsuf," the saladin of the Crusaders, who constructed the citadel in the twelfth century. Two "sakiyehs," worked by oxen, bring the water to the surface.

We now retrace our steps, and are once more reminded of the position England holds in this country by meeting a squad of 'Tommies' ascending to their quarters in Saladin's castle.

CHAPTER VII

The Mosque of Sultan Hasan

We next make for the grey-domed mosque which faces us across the square. Not only is this the finest monument in Cairo, but also the most perfect specimen extant of Saracenic architecture. It was originally built by Sultan Hasan in 1356 to serve as a theological college or "medrêseh," but has since been used as a congregational mosque. We have seen a fine example of the true form of mosque in that of Ibn Tulûn, planned as it is to hold a vast congregation in its spacious inner court. The medrêsehs being intended for the accommodation of scholars, space was not needed for so great a number of worshippers, but more attention had to be given to the requirements of the lecturers and to the housing of the pupils. The dome, which is so important a feature here, as in so many other mosques in Cairo, has nothing to do with the mosque proper, but only exists as a covering to a tomb. So many of the religious monuments in

Cairo serve as the last resting-place of their founders that these domed mausoleums have erroneously come to be considered a necessary feature of a Moslem place of worship.

The cruciform plan of the Sultan Hasan mosque is not seen from the exterior, as the angles are filled in with rooms and offices necessary to a college. The vast wall-space facing the road is therefore only broken when windows are required to light these apartments. The simplicity of this *façade* enhances the grandeur of the cornice which runs around the top of the building. A stalactite ornamentation breaks the horizontal lines at the projection of each course of stones, and the plainness of the wall space below this cornice is enriched by the beautiful shadow cast by it. At noon this shadow sweeps far down the face of the building until we reach the angle where the wall turns more to the sun ; here the shadow shortens as if loath to break the contour of the magnificent portal which we are about to enter.

We ascend a flight of stairs, and from the landing this huge niche rises 66 feet above us. The half-spherical vaulting of the arch is worked up to by twelve tiers of pendentives, delicate little columns round off the angles near the base, and the arched niches that face each other on either side of the door. Beautiful arabesque borders, panels and medallions with delicately-cut geometrical patterns adorn this stately entrance. The original bronze-plated doors were removed by El-Muaiyad to adorn his mosque a century later.

Passing into a domed vestibule and up two passages, we are provided with slippers, that our boots may not defile the floors, and we enter the "salin," or inner courtyard. The four enormous arches which divide this from the transepts impress one more than anything else; their size is, indeed, considerable, but the impression of size they give is far greater. The fountain of ablutions stands, as is customary, in the centre of the open court, and here there is a smaller drinking fountain in addition. The "liwan," or sanctuary, is slightly raised and covered with matting and prayer carpets. The "dikka," or tribune, from which the Koran is read, is of stone, resting on graceful columns. The "mihrab," or "kibla," as the prayer niche is called, is in the centre of the Mekka end of this sanctuary, and next to the stone pulpit.

I was fortunate enough to have made the sketch which is reproduced here as an illustration before the restorations were begun; for, though confident that these are being carried out in the best possible manner, the newness of some of the work will require many years to harmonise it with the older surroundings. Returning to this mosque some ten

W. Tyndale .97

years later, intent on trying to reproduce my first impressions of the court and the great span of the arch which frames in the sanctuary, I was deterred from setting up my easel by the sight of scaffoldings and the noise of workmen. Great cobwebby bits of the frieze, with its Kufic inscriptions, were heaped about on the floor, mouldy slabs of coloured stone had been taken out of the panels to be squared up and cleaned before being cemented into their original places,—a necessary work, no doubt, and it is a blessing that it is directed by such able hands, but it sadly resembles one of those "blessings in disguise," which we are told to be thankful for, when laid low by a severe visitation of Providence! Having gone so far in this work, would that they could go a step further, and rehang the handsome bronze lamps that at various times have been purloined. Some of the best of these are now in the Arab museum, but they would look incomparably better in the surroundings for which they were designed. The arguments I have repeatedly heard,—that valuable objects are liable to be stolen from the mosques—can hardly apply to a lamp weighing about a ton. Some of these, which are ticketed and catalogued in the museum, have been replaced in their legitimate home by lamps that would disgrace a merry-go-round!

A door to the left of the Kibla leads into the

mausoleum of Sultan Hasan, in the centre of which stands his sarcophagus. The dome, which is such a feature from outside, forms the sepulchral canopy. It is a true dome, and if your eye can penetrate the gloom, it can look up the 150 feet that it rises from the ground.

An unworthy monarch was this sultan, who lies in so stately a resting-place. We forgive him a great deal for having raised such a magnificent monument; but we cannot pardon him for the dastardly manner in which he rewarded the genius who designed it. So fearful was he that another might employ his architect to raise a memorial which might eclipse this one, that he ordered the right hand of the designer to be cut off.

In spite of the disturbed times in which this cruel sultan reigned, he was able to devote much time and treasure to building mosques, colleges, and convents. Nineteen, in Cairo alone, are recorded as having been erected by him during the ten years of his rule;—a strange record for a licentious and cruel tyrant. It may be of satisfaction to some that he met with as violent a death as he had so often inflicted on his subjects. A few days before his murder, one of the minarets fell, crushing 300 children in the school below, and one only now remains of the three original minarets which were completed (there were to have been four), and that is the taller of the two now standing. In 1660 the great dome collapsed, and has been replaced by the present one.

During the troublous times of Hasan's later successors, guns were not unfrequently mounted on the terraced roof, from which one faction would try to dislodge another in possession of the citadel; and during peaceful intervals we hear of a tight-rope being stretched from one of the minarets to a citadel bastion, and the Blondin of those days performing on it, to the delight of the crowds assembled in the square.

Facing the Sultan Hasan, stands the unfinished mosque Rifâiyeh, called after a sect of dervishes of that name; which contains the family vault of Ismail Pasha.

We now retrace our steps towards the entrance of the citadel, and descend the Sharia el Magar. A neglected little mosque, with fluted dome nestling close to the minarets, makes a charming picture, whether you look down towards it, or whether you pass it and look up the street towards the citadel mosque just visible in the background. Further down a dilapidated house has crumbled sufficiently to expose an unimportant but delightful tomb mosque, with two stages of its minaret gone. It is a ready-made composition, and a sheltering doorway at the proper distance invites one to sit down and paint it.

It is a cheery-looking bit seen in a blaze of sunshine, though, as these buildings are on the fringe of a great burial-ground, hardly a morning went by while I was at work but several funeral processions wended their way up this street. These are generally headed by a number of poor, and often blind beggars, who dolefully chant the profession of their faith—" La ilâha ill allâh wu Muhammed rasul allâh " ; these are followed by the male relatives of the deceased, dervishes carrying banners, boys singing with their shrill voices verses from the Koran, and the Koran itself carried on a stand and covered with a coloured piece of cloth. The open bier now follows, borne by friends of the departed one. From the head of the bier, which is always foremost, rises a short wooden shaft, surmounted with a turban, if the funeral is that of a man. The women form the rear, the relatives usually having a strip of blue muslin tied round their heads ; they often wave about a piece of blue cloth, while the sobbing of some is drowned in the wailing of others. Professional wailers are often employed ; and the peculiar noise they make is heartrending till one learns that it is done for so much an hour. This is contrary to the laws of the Prophet, but the custom dates back from such a

remote period, that the prohibition has failed to stop it. The men wear no signs of mourning; their argument, that it is selfish and wrong to mourn the loss of one who has died in the faith, and is in consequence in a much happier state than when living, is logical, but apparently not convincing to their sisters, who vie with each other in expressing their grief. Also the existence of professional wailers is hard to reconcile with the argument, as the men would probably have a say in the payment of these women. I put this to my faithful Mohammed. He said that it was wicked, and that these women would burn in hell for it; but with a shrug of his shoulders he seemed to express the uselessness of fighting against an old custom—"Maalesh." As for these wailers themselves, it appears to be but a poor calling indeed—to howl in this world for a wage of a few pence with such awful retribution awaiting them in the next! But that this custom obtained in very early times is evidenced by some of the wall paintings in the tombs at Thebes.

However, while ensconced in this doorway I have watched the funeral of some noted saint go by, when the dead silence was only broken at intervals by a low repetition of some text of the Koran. It was much more impressive, and a great relief, for these screaming women soon got on my nerves. The peculiar upright shaft at the head of the bier, like a flagstaff at the stern of a ship, bears some sign of the nationality or status of the deceased. During the obsequies of the saint I noticed that this staff carried a green turban. The number of dervishes was greater, and the quantity of banners showed that most of the sects were represented.

To the left of our illustration rises the minaret of the Mosque of Aksunkur, which is well worth a visit. Built by one of the sons of en-Nasir, in the middle of the fourteenth century, it was restored by Ibrâhîm Agha 300 years later. It is now known by the name of the latter and is often called the "Blue mosque," from the colour of the tiles which Ibrahim used in its internal decoration. It is this mass of beautiful tiles which, more than anything else, draws painters to this shrine. During the hot weather the large surfaces of blue, tending towards green in places and violet in others, make one forget, to a certain extent, the height of the thermometer; and the prevailing colour of the heated streets, a warm buff with touches of red, makes these cool shades doubly attractive.

The sanctuary of all mosques is at the south-east, or Mekka end, and obtains its light through the open colonnade in the opposite direction; the sun's rays, therefore, do not enter here till late in the day, when they have lost their power; save, now and again, when a little patch of light from a clerestory window climbs slowly up a column and imparts to it the hue of the tiny bits of glass it filters through. It is therefore very much cooler than the sun-baked court which we cross to reach it. One can dispense with the slippers that the attendant wishes to fit over one's boots, for it is gratifying to have so good an excuse to go barefooted; and, away from the street, one's coat and waistcoat can also be dispensed with.

It is well to work in some other part of the building during the time of prayer; the palms casting their shadows over the domed fountain make a pretty sketch, and the blue-tiled chamber, where the sarcophagus of Aksunkur lies, is one of the most pictorial bits in Cairo. During the winter a sunny corner of the open court is often selected by a teacher to hold his class in, or more often it is used by some unemployed for the mid-day nap. Little children will play about here while their elders are at their devotions, and doves circle around and drink from the overflow of the fountain—when the kestrels are not using the minaret as a point of vantage. We may learn patience from the mosque cat, as he sits watching a crack in the wall on the chance of securing a too venturesome mouse ; a chirp from a sparrow, in whose movements he also takes a kindly interest, may divert his eyes for a moment ; but, with an unspoken—" I'll attend to you presently," he directs them again to the all-engrossing hole in the wall.

The " sala " concluded, we may return to the sanctuary, while the worshippers pick up their slippers, which lie on the step that descends to the court, and carry them to the entrance, where they put them on and return to their various advocations. Except on Fridays, there appears to be no one to lead the services; the men fall into rows before the " Kibleh," and go through certain prostrations in a given order, while reciting the prescribed verses of the Koran. Women never attend these prayers, which probably accounts for the fallacious idea, held in Europe, that Mohammedans consider that women have no souls. A Moslem might almost equally argue that the English believe that women alone have them, if he were to witness some of our services where the ladies form nearly the whole of the congregation. The social relations of the sexes oblige the women to say their prayers apart from the men, but they have to keep the fast of Ramadân as strictly as their brothers ; which would be the refinement of cruelty if they have no souls

to benefit by it. So strict is this fast that they may only break it when they are nursing a child, and they have to make up for it when the child is weaned. A few will occasionally steal into a mosque, when the men are away, to visit the shrine of some favourite saint, and one of these which has some miraculous power of curing barrenness is especially favoured.

The street which this mosque is in is a particularly interesting one ; not so much on account of any especial monuments, but that the houses seem to have suffered less from European influence, and one can enjoy these all the more as it is not a very crowded thoroughfare. When we reach the mosque of El-Merdani we are on familiar ground, and the beautiful Muaiyad minarets soon come into sight. Leaving the Bâb Zuwêlêh on our right, after just glancing to see if the holy man of the rags and the spear still sits there, we notice on our left an unpretentious little mosque entrance at the top of a stairway. I say "mosque," because it is the custom to call most places connected with Mohammedan worship by that name ; but what the building actually is I have never been able to learn. We enter, cross a little cloister, and two or three more steps take us into an ideal courtyard. Two sides are covered with tiles, and in the centre of one is a pretty "Kibleh," or praying niche, which is the only sign that one is in a religious enclosure ; some trees, and the backs of the houses of the tent-bazaar, rise above this ; and veiled women pass in and out and disappear behind the wall with the praying niche.

While I painted this the faithful Mohammed informed me that a saint was buried there and that these ladies said their prayers around his shrine ; but more than this I could not find out. There might possibly have been the prettiest subject for my brush behind those tiles, but I concluded that it would be indiscreet to investigate further. No guide-books, or works on Arab architecture, say a word about this quaint and charming spot ; and perhaps this is just as well, for it is a pearl that should not be cast before,—well, let us say, any but those who are able to appreciate its beauty.

From here we can join the Avenue Mohammed Ali, near the Arab museum, and so return to the heart of the European quarter.

CHAPTER VIII

Another Ramble in Old Cairo

Starting from the "Rond Point" up the Muski soon after that thoroughfare has been crossed by the Khalîg, we can work our way to the left into the Derb-el-Yehûdîyeh, which is the main street traversing the Jewish quarter. Though not restricted to a ghetto as in former times, the same race still inhabit this part of Cairo. The appearance of the houses and of their inmates differs but slightly from that of the Arab quarters. A few more men in European dress may be seen, but these are probably only there on business, and live in the more modern parts of Cairo. Younger women have ceased to veil their faces now the Moslem has become used to seeing the "Firangi" ladies, and it is therefore less of a shock to his sense of decency; but until recent years both the Coptic and Jewish women wore the "yashmak"; not, of course, as a religious obligation, but as a protection. The Cairene shows more traces of Semitic blood than the " fellah " ; it is therefore chiefly by some slight difference in the dress, which custom rather than any sumptuary law has imposed, that one can distinguish the Jew from the Moslem. Arabic—their language in common—being much akin to Hebrew, is spoken by both people with the same accent ; yet, slight as the differences are, the Arab can always detect the Yehûdî, even when the latter has embraced Mohammedanism.

The Jewish quarter lies at the back of the goldsmiths' bazaar which we entered on another occasion from the Nahâssîn. We pass this on our right and soon enter a dilapidated courtyard of thc Mûristan of Kalâûn. By a curious chance, a modern dispensary has been set up here, and the sick people awaiting their turn to have their ailments attended to by an up to date native doctor, can recall the time when this Mûristan was the great hospital of Cairo.

Saladin had anticipated the great work of the sultan Kalâûn by more than a century. The Spanish Arab, Ibn Gubeyr, who visited Cairo in the twelfth century, gives a detailed account of it, and, in the able translation of his travels by Mr. Guy Le Strange, we read that Saladin "was prompted to the meritorious deed of establishing this hospital solely by the hope of gaining favour with God and recompense in the world to come."

W. Tyndale

"This great palace, spacious and magnificent," to once more quote the Spaniard, could not long have outlasted the good sultan, for all we see of the present building was erected by Kalâûn during the following century. Parts are in a very ruinous condition, but one can still trace some of the wards set aside for the various diseases known at that time.

A lofty corridor leads to the imposing portal facing the coppersmiths' bazaar. To the left of this great passage you enter the vestibule of the tomb of the founder. This is at present in the hands of the restorer, as well as the tomb chamber. Both lend themselves especially to pictorial treatment; the simplicity of the vestibule with the green wooden arcade is as tempting to paint as the rich, sombre colour of the great mausoleum. Groups of students are often to be seen in the former, squatting on the matting and listening to some "ulema" expounding texts from the Koran. Near the tomb hang some of Kalâûn's garments, which are believed to possess miraculous healing powers, and many sick people would give this cure a trial before resorting to the "Firangi-taught" hakim in charge of the modern dispensary in the courtyard.

The prayer recess is perhaps the most beautiful one in Cairo; it appeared to be in a fairly good state of preservation when I attempted to paint it a few years ago, so we may hope that the workmen may soon cease to disturb the solemnity of the place.

The Mûristan Kalâûn is the most important monument of the latter part of the thirteenth century ; that it should be carefully preserved is all important ; and the sound judgment shown by Herz Bey in most of the work committed to his care, leads one to hope that preservation rather than restoration is what is being done in this case.

Passing through the black and white marble portal, we will follow the Nahâssîn till we get to the Sebîl of Abd-er-Rahmân, leaving the handsome tomb-mosques of Bâb-en-Nasr and Barkûk on our left. Here we shall again enjoy the perspective of this enchanting street before diving down the narrow lanes leading to the Gamâlîyeh. A camel laden with tumbâk, the coarse kind of tobacco smoked in the nargîlehs, may so completely block the way, that, if you cannot duck under the panniers, you may have to seek refuge in some doorway until the brute has gone by. One or two larger khâns in these narrow streets appear to have fallen on bad times, for the cigarette is replacing the nargîleh, and the tumbâkiyeh shows signs that its trade has drifted into other channels. A mosque, at the corner before you turn into the Gamâlîyeh street, is in such a state of disrepair that it looks as if the tumbâk merchant thought that his business was past praying for.

The main street we are now in has much of the life and bustle of the Nahâssîn, but all is on a poorer scale. The shops look less prosperous, the silk robes of the merchants are replaced by the blue cotton galabieh, and the distinguished beauty of the street we have left is replaced by a rugged picturesqueness. At an angle to the road, the entrance to a spacious khân makes a good vantage ground for a sketch, while a stone seat on either side of the gateway looks as though placed there on purpose to accommodate a sketching stool, which probably accounts for the many times this Gamâlîyeh has been painted. One is slightly raised above the heads of the people while the angle of the wall protects one from an inquisitive crowd in the rear. Even when not painting this street with the mosque of Bîbars rising in the centre of the picture, it is a useful corner from which to make rapid studies of the people as they approach or recede from one.

I witnessed a curious incident when I was last ensconced in this doorway. A man was leading a camel and calling out to every shopman as he passed. The beast bore no load, so I could not think what the man was hawking. Occasionally someone would stop him, and appear to take an interest in the animal's neck, while another would feel his hump or thighs ; it then dawned upon me that the camel was for sale, but not till he got near me did I realise that the brute was being sold piecemeal, and that its different joints were bespoken, and scored and initialled with a bit of chalk. What relation the price per pound of the best part of the neck bore to the price of a pound of hump I was unable to ascertain. This cold-blooded proceeding made me resolve to become a vegetarian, a resolution to which, except at meal times, I have strictly adhered.

As we proceed along the Gamâlîyeh the signs of decay are more and more manifest. Fine old houses are tenanted by the poorest of people, the meshrebiya has dropped from most of the bay windows, which are either roughly boarded up, or disfigured by bits of sacking to keep out the draught; great ragged awnings float across the road, where some shopman still has some goods worth protecting from the rays of the sun. The houses in the side streets are yet more ruinous than those in the main thoroughfare. This appearance of decay, which one sees here and in so large a part of Cairo, is hard to reconcile with the increased prosperity of Egypt, of which one hears so much.

The Gamâlîyeh ends at the Bâb-en-Nasr, the gate of victory, which, together with the Bâb-el-Futûh, or gate of capture, was built during the latter part

of the 11th century by the famous vizier Bedr el-Gamali. The mosque of Hâkim, dating from a century earlier, nearly fills up the space between these two gates. Napoleon quartered some of his troops here in 1799, fully realising the strength of the position.

These two gates, together with the Bâb Zuwêleh, have puzzled a good many archæologists. Their style is not Saracenic; it savours more of the Norman. M. van Berchem, who has made a special study of the old enceinte of the city, describes them as of the Templars' style of military architecture, but as they were erected some ten years before the date of the first crusade, this influence upon their style seems extraordinary. Van Berchem discovered Greek mason's marks, which accord with their Byzantine appearance, and, as the great vizier Bedr was an Armenian, it is probable that he sought his architect among his own countrymen. We are, however, more concerned with their pictorial aspect; and, impressive as they are, it is difficult to give a satisfactory presentment of them.

The ruined mosque of el-Hâkim that fills most of the angle in the city wall, connecting the two gates, is a capital sketching ground. It is of itself less impressive than that of Ibn Tulûn, which it resembles in plan; but, being more accessible to the outside world, one can use the great courtyard as a setting for groups of camels, Bedouin tents, or much else of the furnishing of an oriental picture. Its name of el-Hâkim doubtlessly adds to the interest of the place. I feel sorely tempted to purloin the account of that extraordinary caliph which Stanley Lane Poole gives in his *Story of Cairo*, but as this delightful book is within easy reach of anyone visiting Egypt, I cannot do better than recommend it to my readers.

In a vacant space, outside the Bâb-en-Nasr, and adjoining a large Mohammedan cemetery, one can often watch the antics of "Karakush," who corresponds to our Punch. Under the shadow of the old wall a motley crowd form a circle around the performers, who generally comprise a man, a small boy, a dog, and a monkey. A free use of the stick keeps the small boys from encroaching on the area that "Karakush" considers necessary for the performance. The jokes, which may date from the Moslem invasion of Egypt, have lost nothing of their zest from constant repetition, and it does one's heart good to hear the roars of laughter of the audience. These witticisms are coarser than would be permitted at an English seaside resort, but they must be judged from another standpoint. What is hidden or only hinted at with us, is here considered an innocent form of amusement; and broad as the jests often are, they are refinement itself compared to what may be heard and seen in the more modern part of Cairo. " Karakush," whose very name now brings a smile to the face of a Cairene, was, however, not a comical personage in his day ; for he is described as one of Saladin's most faithful emirs, and we hear of his doing nothing more humorous than repelling crusaders, whose uninvited visits he considered an impertinence.

Merry-go-rounds, that might serve as models in Punch's Prehistoric Peeps, are often set up here ; and on religious festivals large tents project from the walls, in which the people, who have had their laugh at " Karakush's " ribald antics, may witness a Zikr. A dozen or more dervishes will here form into line, and, taking the lead from one of them, will slowly sway backwards and forwards, repeating the name of Allah. The movement gradually gets faster and more violent, the performers seem to lose all consciousness of their surroundings, until, having reached the limits of physical endurance, they will fall out and lie about as if in an ecstatic trance.

The great cemetery which borders on this open space, and actually invades it here and there, in no way detracts from the hilarity of the crowd. It is unenclosed, and tombstones may serve as seats, or for small boys to practise leap-frog. Amongst these graves is that of Burckhardt, the oriental traveller, who died in 1817. To the Arabs he was known as the Sheykh Ibrahim.

Following the city wall for some two or three hundred yards in an easterly direction, when it turns sharply to the south, we leave the cemetery and skirt round the rubbish mounds, pass the domed tomb of Sheykh Galal on our left, and the so-called Tombs of the Caliphs come into view. It is an impressive sight, this city of the dead, whether seen in a mid-day blaze of sunshine, or towards evening when the rosy light from the west just catches the domes and minarets, while the ruinous buildings at their base are lost in the violet shade of the rubbish hills. It is worth climbing the nearest of these hills to get a more comprehensive view of these tombs. Though a city dedicated to the dead, it was not always, as at present, a dead city ; for each mosque tomb had sufficient endowment to keep several attendants, who were housed close by.

The ruins of khâns are here also, suggesting that some trades were carried on, and that the baths and fountains were intended to supply the wants of a considerable population. They were built during the thirteenth and two following centuries, as the mausoleums of the Bahrite and Circassian Mamelukes who were then ruling Egypt. The earlier Caliphs were mostly buried

in what is, at present, the centre of Cairo, but what, in their days, was outside their capital, which lay to the south, and of which very few vestiges now remain. The Khan Khalîl now stands on the site of this earlier burial place ; and we are told that when it was built the bones of the Caliphs were dug up, carried away on asses' backs, and shot on to the rubbish hills.

One of the first tombs we approach,—el-Seb'a Benat, "the seven sisters,"—is evidence that others besides Mamelukes lay here, but who these seven ladies were I have not been able to discover. As space does not allow of an examination of more than the outside of these tombs, we will make for one on the eastern side of the group ; that of the Sultan Kâit Bey. The tomb of Sultan Barkûk, on our left, has two beautiful domes and a pair of minarets. It is worth making a careful study of the designs on each of the many domes as we pass along. The general plan of each tomb differs slightly ; but, on close examination, one is surprised to find how varied the detail is. The mausoleum of Kâit Bey is the finest here, and its slender minaret and beautifully decorated dome surpass all others. It has all the appointments of a congregational mosque ; the fountain, surmounted by the arcaded school-room, to the left of the high entrance, which has handsome bronze-mounted doors ; the central open court, the 'lîwân,' or sanctuary, with prayer-rugs and pulpit, on the Mekka side; and finally the domed sepulchre of the Sultan. Though built a century after Saracenic architecture had reached its highest level, it may still be considered one of the gems of Cairo.

Working our way from here, either round or over the mounds of rubbish, we reach the Sharia esh-Sharawâni,—the continuation of the Muski, and so return to the European quarter.

A tramway runs from el-Ataba Khadrâ, near the central post office, to what is known as Old Cairo or Masr-el-Atîka ; it passes down the Boulevard Abd-ul-Aziz, then takes a turn towards the Nile ; and from where the Kasr-en-Nîl bridge crosses the river we follow its course to within some two or three hundred yards of where the line ends. The trees and flowering shrubs help to disguise the ugliness of the modern villas that we pass on the way, but what we see of Old Cairo from the tramway is less interesting than much that we have seen in parts of Cairo even more deserving of the title old.

We walk up the bazaar to the left of the main road, cross the railway, and at the end of a narrow little lane we pass through a gateway in the encircling wall of the Roman fortress of Babylon. Dilapidated buildings hide too much of the remains of the castle to enable us to appreciate its importance. The inhabitants of this quarter seem shy of strangers; possibly an inherited fear of an unwelcome visit from the alien people outside their enclosure. However, through some grating we have been recognised as being nothing more alarming than "Sawarhine," and a prospect of backsheesh brings out some of the inhabitants, who follow us through this warren till we reach the church of St. George, or Mâri Girgis.

There is so much similarity in the conditions in which these people live and that of the dwellers in a Moorish "mellah" (the Arabic Ghetto), that it would not have surprised me if our followers had had a Jewish type of countenance, instead of a complete absence of the Semitic features which are so common amongst the Arabs.

The Copts, into whose quarters we are intruding, are Egyptian of the Egyptians. Their very name, derived from the Greek "Aiguptios" and contracted into the Arabic "Kupt," helps to prove this.

Of all the dwellers in the Nile valley these are the ones which appeal most to our sympathy, and it is pleasant to think that, after centuries of oppression, they can enjoy a full measure of freedom under the British occupation of their country.

CHAPTER IX

In the Copts' Quarter

Before we enter the Coptic church of St. George, it is interesting to hark back to the days when the Copts forswore the cult of Osiris and were received into the fold of the Christian Church.

As far back as A.D. 62 Armianus was appointed bishop of Alexandria, and, during the patriarchate of Demetrius, a century later, Christian communities which are associated with the names of Clement, Origen, and Pantænus sprang up all over the Delta. The third century saw the rise of the monastic system, and from the Delta to the confines of Nubia the ruins of early monasteries show how rapidly the new religion took hold of the people. Besides these ruined convents there is hardly a temple that does not bear witness to the religious zeal of these early Christians. Far distant from Rome as they were, they probably suffered less from persecution than did their brethren who were nearer the seat of empire; but, at this period, quarrels amongst themselves did more to impede their religion than the persecutions of any Roman emperor. The teachings of Arius, a presbyter of Alexandria, influenced the majority in spite of the exhortations of their Bishop Alexander and the eloquence of his deacon Athanasius. At the Council of Nice in 325, which the latter attended, Arianism was condemned, and Christians in Egypt were ranged in two hostile camps. We do not know whether this controversy was of much interest to Constantine personally, but his son Constantius, who succeeded him, threw in his lot with the Arians. Athanasius was deposed and exiled, and his followers were persecuted by the Arians, but an Edict of Theodosius in 379 declared the Orthodox Church to be the State religion of Egypt; and the Arians again suffered their turn of persecution. A national church now rose side by side with the State church, and after the Council of Chalcedon in 451 the former fell away entirely from the latter. The nationalists, who were the larger party, were known as Jacobites, or Copts, and the orthodox were known in Egypt as the Melekites. By the time of the invasion of Egypt by Amr, the Caliph Omar's great general, the Copts were ready to throw in their lot with any one who might free them from the tyranny of their Byzantine governors. We shall have more to say of Amr presently.

There is nothing in the exterior of the church of St. George to suggest the richness of its interior decoration, and this applies to the six other churches hidden away in this fortress. To escape notice, and to avoid any display that might awaken the cupidity of their neighbours, is the explanation given by some for this simple exterior, but as the exteriors of the earliest mosques were equally plain, there is nothing peculiar in this feature. With the exception of the crypt, which dates previous to the Moslem conquest, this church was built not long after Ibn-Tulûn had completed his great mosque, and nothing could be plainer than the outside of the latter. The person who unbolts the massive door takes care to shut out the rest of our followers, for it is just as well not to share the baksheesh with too many. We cross a small vestibule, which screens the interior from the outside should the door happen to be open, and enter a beautiful little basilica, two rows of arches separate the aisles from the nave, which appears short to our eyes, for a handsome wooden screen divides the church in two at some distance from the sanctuary. The dim light from the small triforium windows is caught by a row of saints above the screen ; it is reflected here and there on the gold halo of an ikon, and flickers down the carved woodwork. During the services the women must keep to the

rear side of this screen; the further side being reserved for the men.

Leaving the nave and passing into what corresponds to a choir we face three altars, each standing in a circular apse and surmounted by a dome. Screens again hide these altars, and that which veils the high altar is more delicate in design and richer in material than any other; its lattice work is formed of little crosses carved in ebony and ivory. During the celebration of the Mass these doors are opened and the curtain is withdrawn, and a large image of Christ is seen above the altar. The coloured ostrich eggs which hang from the ceiling form a curious decoration. These are occasionally seen in mosques, and are also used to adorn the chapel of St. Helena in the church of the Holy Sepulchre at Jerusalem.

A flight of steps in the choir lead down to the crypt, in which we are shown a seat upon which the Holy Family rested on their journey to Egypt. There was some difficulty in getting permission to sketch in any of these Coptic churches, and it was not until I was staying at the excavators' camp at Abydos that I was able to do so.

A small Christian colony inhabits an early dynasty fort in the desert west of the temple of Seti, which is known as the Coptic convent. Baedeker contemptuously dismisses it as unworthy of a visit. The relation which that church bears to the one we are now in, is much the same as that of a picturesque old country parish church to an elaborate cathedral, but I found it worthy of a good many visits, even with the thermometer at a hundred in the shade. When inside the old fort there was much to recall the aspect of the interior of the fortress of Babylon; some fowls scratching about a midden and a few cattle sheds imparted a flavour of the country that is absent here, but the same stillness, the same almost windowless houses are common to both places. The kindly old priest who showed me round seemed so much a part of the basilica that I found it hard to realise that I was talking to a contemporary. His dress and surroundings all savoured so much of the middle ages that I felt as though I had slept and wakened up six centuries earlier. The fort inside which this church and cluster of houses stand belongs to the early empire; it stood there 3,000 years before the convent was built, but as there were no signs of human activity visible to mark the centuries, time seemed stationary. The priest interested me as much as his surroundings; the little world in which he and his family live is all sufficient to supply their needs, and an occasional journey to Balliana, the town on the Nile bank ten miles away, brings him sufficiently in touch with the doings of the outside world to enable him to appreciate the peaceful happiness of his remote village. "Salâm Alekûm!" both to the padre and to his flock.

If time allows it is well worth while to visit all the six churches in Babylon. The name given by the Greeks to the Roman fortress is a puzzle to archæologists; it is suggested that it may be an imitation of one of the names given to the eastern suburb of Memphis which stood here at a remote age; but this seems vague. The massive towers and bastions, and what one can still see of the walls, is all that visibly remains of the old city of Misr. Old Cairo, or Masr el-Atika, which lies between us and the river, dates later than the thirteenth century, for, till then, its site and that of the modern quarters of Cairo was all under water.

Most of Egypt fell an easy prey to Amr, who, we are told, invaded it with only 4,000 troopers, and the Copts, possibly not realising that the Moslems had come to stay, were glad of this help to free them from the tyranny of the orthodox Byzantines. The taking of this castle was another matter, for here the representatives of the Empire were supreme. Amr had to be heavily reinforced, and not till after a seven months' siege was he able to reduce this stronghold. From April, 641, when this fateful event took place,

Egypt has formed a part of the Mohammedan world.

But the Copts soon discovered that they had merely changed masters : the rule of the Moslem was possibly gentler than that of their fellow-Christians—the slight difference of whose doctrines perhaps few could understand—but, cut off from the support of the mother church, there remained but little earthly help for them to look to when less tolerant rulers succeeded Amr. Many of the weaker brethren must have safeguarded their lives and property by embracing the dominant faith, and others must have fallen in defending the creed of their fathers. The remnant is now not more than a tenth of the population of Egypt ; but when we consider how the Saracens suffered from the repeated crusades, we wonder that any have been able to survive the vengeance of Islam. Many of them now hold high positions in the Government, and their business aptitude fits them well for the places they fill in most of the public offices.

On leaving the " Kasr esh-Shêma," as the Arabs term this fortress, we skirt round a part of the walls and cross the rubbish heaps that separate us from Amr's mosque. These rubbish heaps are all that remain of Fostât, the first town the Moslem invaders built in Egypt ; still less is visible of the

earlier Misr which surrounded Babylon and lay at the edge of the Nile whose waters have receded to their present course.

It is not within the scope of this volume to give a history of Egypt during the middle ages ; and it would be presumptuous to attempt what has been so ably done of late by Stanley Lane Poole ; but as our walk now appeals more to any archæological tastes we may have than to our æsthetic ones, a few words on the growth and extension of Cairo may not be out of place.

When Amr lay siege to the castle which we are leaving behind us, he pitched his tent on the spot where his mosque now stands, and a pretty story is told of how this spot became especially endeared to him. After Babylon had surrendered, Amr prepared to leave for Alexandria, which still held out for the Emperor Heraclius, and soldiers were sent to strike his tent. A dove sitting on its nest attracted the attention of these men, who reported it to their general. Amr ordered that the bird should not be disturbed, and the tent was still found standing when he and his army returned after the taking of Alexandria. This spot was henceforth considered sacred, and Egypt's first mosque commemorates this simple event.

El-Fostât, or "the town of the Tent," is the nucleus of the great city that has risen north of this mosque. The waste of land encumbered with débris, that separates Fostât from Cairo as we know it, was formerly occupied by a faubourg of the original town, El-Askar, or "the cantonments," which arose after the Omayad caliphs were superseded by the Abbasids in 750. The Governor built his palace here, and it soon bore the same relation to Fostât as the West-end bears to the city of London. Further north stretched the wards allotted to the different nationalities that formed part of the Emir's retinue. It was when Ibn-Tulûn came to Egypt to govern it as the representative of the first Turkish caliph in 868 that these wards were chosen as the site for his government house. El-Askar stretched to the hill of Yeshkur, beyond which rise the walls of the present capital, enclosing Tulûn's mosque, of which we have spoken. Fostât and El-Askar lost consequence as the new royal suburb arose, and nothing now stands of either to testify to their importance save this ruinous mosque. El Katai, or "the wards," fared little better; it became a town the splendour of which Arab historians never tire in relating; its site is covered with houses of a much more recent growth, and only the deserted mosque that bears his name remains of the glorious faubourg which Ibn Tulûn built, and that his son Khumâruyeh beautified. The descriptions of the palace, the "Golden House," the "summer pavilion," or "dome of the air," and the gardens and fountains, probably inspired the writers of the *Arabian Nights* more than the actual surroundings of Haroun al-Raschid, which were less luxurious than those of his successors.

Though Amr built the first mosque in Egypt, that which we see now standing has probably not a square foot of the original structure in it. "The Crown of Mosques," as the Arab warriors called the first place of worship that they erected in their newly-conquered country, was a poor looking structure compared to what these people have built since they assimilated the art of the Copts and became largely influenced by the culture of their Turkish rulers. It was rebuilt on a much larger scale nearly two centuries later, and restored in 1798 by Murad Bey. Most of what we now see is therefore of the ninth century; so it may still claim to be Cairo's oldest mosque. The marble columns supporting the huge arcade were the spoil from existing or ruined Christian churches, and their not matching each other seemed to have troubled these early builders very little; a little shortening of one, or lengthening of another, made them suit their purpose; they might, however, have taken a little more care, and have placed all the capitals the right way up!

Guides will point out the column in front of the pulpit, with the "Kurbûg" of the prophet drawn by the veins in the grey marble, and they will tell you how this column flew through the air from the Kaaba at Mekka to help Amr in building his mosque. They are somewhat out in their chronology, but these stories are interesting. It is prophesied the fall of Islam will coincide with the fall of this mosque, but from its poor state of repair, the faithful must take this with a grain of salt.

There is not much to detain us here. The vast court with the fountain in the centre is very impressive, but its historical associations can be studied at home in an arm-chair.

A walk or donkey ride from here to the tombs of the Mamelukes in a north-easterly direction is charming. As the sun sinks in the west, the light catches the citadel mosque, which looks well at a distance, also the Mokattam hills, with the little mosque of Giyûshi beyond. A pale, broad shadow slowly creeps across the foreground, and ugly details are lost in its subduing effect. The deepening colour of the sun's rays turns these hills from gold to orange, until they are finally lost in a roseate reflection of the afterglow.

The Tombs of the Mamelukes are less interesting than those we have seen of the

so-called Caliphs, but a walk past them at the approach of twilight is a thing to be long remembered. We enter the town at the Bâb el-Karâfeh and the tramway will take us back to the Ezbekîyeh.

CHAPTER X

The Pyramids

The great event after arriving in Cairo is the excursion to the pyramids. No one can fail to have an idea of their appearance, and all can learn their age and dimensions, for nothing ever raised by human energy has been more written about. None, however, can feel the awe their size produces till they reach the plateau on which the mighty tomb of Cheops stands. One is gradually worked up to this feeling from the moment when they first come into sight on the five mile road from Gîzeh. At first they appear so small compared with the objects in the near foreground; after a mile or two one looks again, and the sense of disappointment which the first glance provoked has hardly lessened. Their size increases as one is driven nearer, but not to the extent one is led to expect. Things look more hopeful as the carriage reaches the limits of the cultivated land, and upon arriving at the higher level, where one alights at the edge of the desert, the size of the Great Pyramid begins to take hold of one. This increases at an abnormal rate, as step by step one ascends the plateau on which it stands, where a sense of hugeness becomes overwhelming. The colour helps this impression ; that of the rock and sand on which the pyramid rests is carried upward, and blocks out most of the sky, till, nearing the zenith, the pale gold tells out boldly against the deep blue.

Would that one could be allowed to enjoy these novel sensations in peace ! But the Bedouin Arabs, who have settled here so long that they have lost their nomadic instincts, are not disposed to allow their prey to enjoy quietly what they consider their property. Should it be out of the tourist season, each one looks for a picking from the rare stranger ; but in mid-winter, when the "Sawarhine" flock here in great numbers, one may be subjected to the attentions of only one or two of these pests. One has read up all, and much more, than they can tell one in their broken English, and, at moments when one's own thoughts and impressions are quite sufficing, uninvited information is very exasperating. They are handsome, picturesque looking fellows, and if they left one alone their presence might be acceptable, as they harmonise with the surroundings, and help to scale the size of what one has come to see. They seem not to resent being told to go away, long usage has accustomed them to that ; but, go where you will, they will follow you about until every sense but one of irritation has left one. Some attempt has recently been made to lessen this nuisance, but it has been a great failure, as far as my own personal experience has gone. Possibly in the full season they may be kept more in check now than formerly.

To enjoy the pyramids the full season is the time of the year to avoid, if it is possible. Tourists disputing with extortionate camel drivers or donkey boys, bargaining for sham scarabs, standing in parties to be photographed, or preparing their lunch, might all be very entertaining if watched from a hotel terrace in Cairo, but this is not what one has come here to see. Before or after the season one is spared these irrelevancies, but the control of the Bedouin is at all times very much relaxed. I have been informed of the share which the police, who are stationed there to keep order, get in order that they should not interfere with these pests when on their hunt for baksheesh. I have often heard these creatures defended, as not being so bad as they are made out to be, but this advocacy is generally from the fair sex ; and it is possible that were these fine-looking fellows replaced by equally good-looking women, the men might not condemn them so sweepingly. To buy up the village where these people live, and to transplant the population elsewhere has been suggested as the only efficacious remedy. However, the Antiquities Department, which would be expected to do this, has not enough income to carry out its present work, and it certainly could not spare the money to execute this reform. Egypt is well policed, and it should be the duty of the police to stop this nuisance. The visitors, who are the ones to suffer, stay too short a while in the country to agitate in the matter, but the foreign residents in Cairo could do so; unfortunately they suffer less persecution, as their knowledge of Arabic distinguishes them from the "Sawarhine"; they therefore do not trouble about the matter.

This is a long digression, but this nuisance is now so much a part of a visit to the pyramids that it is difficult not to allude to it. By simulating deafness you may succeed in stopping the chatter of your followers, but to shake them off is not possible.

A stroll along the base of Cheop's great tomb helps one to realise its size. You walk a distance of 260 yards before reaching the angle, then look along the next face, and the same length is before you; and, should you feel inclined to walk round the four sides, you will have covered a distance of just under three-quarters of a mile. Thirteen acres does this base cover : something more than the whole square of Lincoln's Inn Fields.

The great blocks of stone that are superimposed in receding layers, and which appeared like bricks from the road, contain forty cubic feet, and, according to the calculations of Professor Flinders Petrie, 2,300,000 of these blocks were required to construct this pyramid. Imagination fails to stretch back sixty centuries to the time of its raising. Stonework weathers very little in the desert, therefore the colour does not help you. It is true that what we see has only been exposed to the elements for five centuries, when the outer casing was taken to be utilised for building material in Cairo, about the time that Hasan's mosque was erected. It is only a wonder that such a convenient quarry, with ready-faced stones, had not been worked even earlier.

The waste of human energy in raising such a tomb is appalling. Professor Flinders Petrie, in defending this, states that the workmen were only put on during the high Nile, when their agricultural pursuits would of necessity be stopped : but the time of the flood is the most trying time of the year, and it is a mistake to think that the native does not feel the heat. The "fellah," who has changed very little physically during these sixty centuries, and is naturally a hard worker, slacks off a good deal when the excessive heat sets in. We remember that the labourers in the vineyard who had "borne the burden and heat of the day" appear not to have liked it, though the heat of the day in Palestine is not nearly so oppressive as it is during the late summer in Egypt. Herodotus relates that, to build this pyramid, the labour of one hundred thousand men was required during a space of twenty years, and Flinders Petrie does not consider that this is an over estimate. To feed and discipline such an army of workmen shows a wonderful power of organisation ; while the work of quarrying these stones in the Mokattam Hills, ten miles away, bringing them here and adjusting them with such marvellous precision proves a high state of civilisation, which is hard to reconcile with the senselessness of this unproductive undertaking.

I am told that the contractor for the Assuan dam amused himself, while staying at Mena House, in making out an estimate of what it would cost him, with the present-day machinery at his disposal, to build the Great Pyramid. This worked out at six millions. Also it would be interesting to know what it would work out at, if only the appliances of the fourth Dynasty were used.

We have spoken so far of only one pyramid, but you will find that, though the second one of

Khephren is nearly as important, and that besides the three principal ones there are six smaller ones, this one will have exhausted all your resources of awe and wonderment. Of the "seven wonders of the world" this group of pyramids is the greatest and the oldest, and the only one of the number that we are still privileged to see.

We descend the shelving plateau a little to the south and hurry on to view the further side of a great mass of stone before us, where a colossal pair of shoulders, surmounted by a wig, rises up against the sky as we get lower into the surrounding hollow. We skirt along the edge of this little valley and turn round, and the huge head of the Sphinx stands out sharply against the wonderful blue of the sky.

Nose and part of the upper lip are gone, and also the beard. The general outline of the shoulders remains, but no detail is seen in the mass that supports the head but the stratifications of the rock out of which this titanic bust was hewn. A broken stone causeway proceeds from the right of this mass, and if we stand at a proper distance to take in the whole, we can distinguish the outline of a forearm and the outstretched fingers of a hand. The battered features of this colossus rivet our attention, if we are fortunate enough to be spared the chatter of the pyramid pests. The drawing of the lips and eyes are still sufficiently clearly defined to

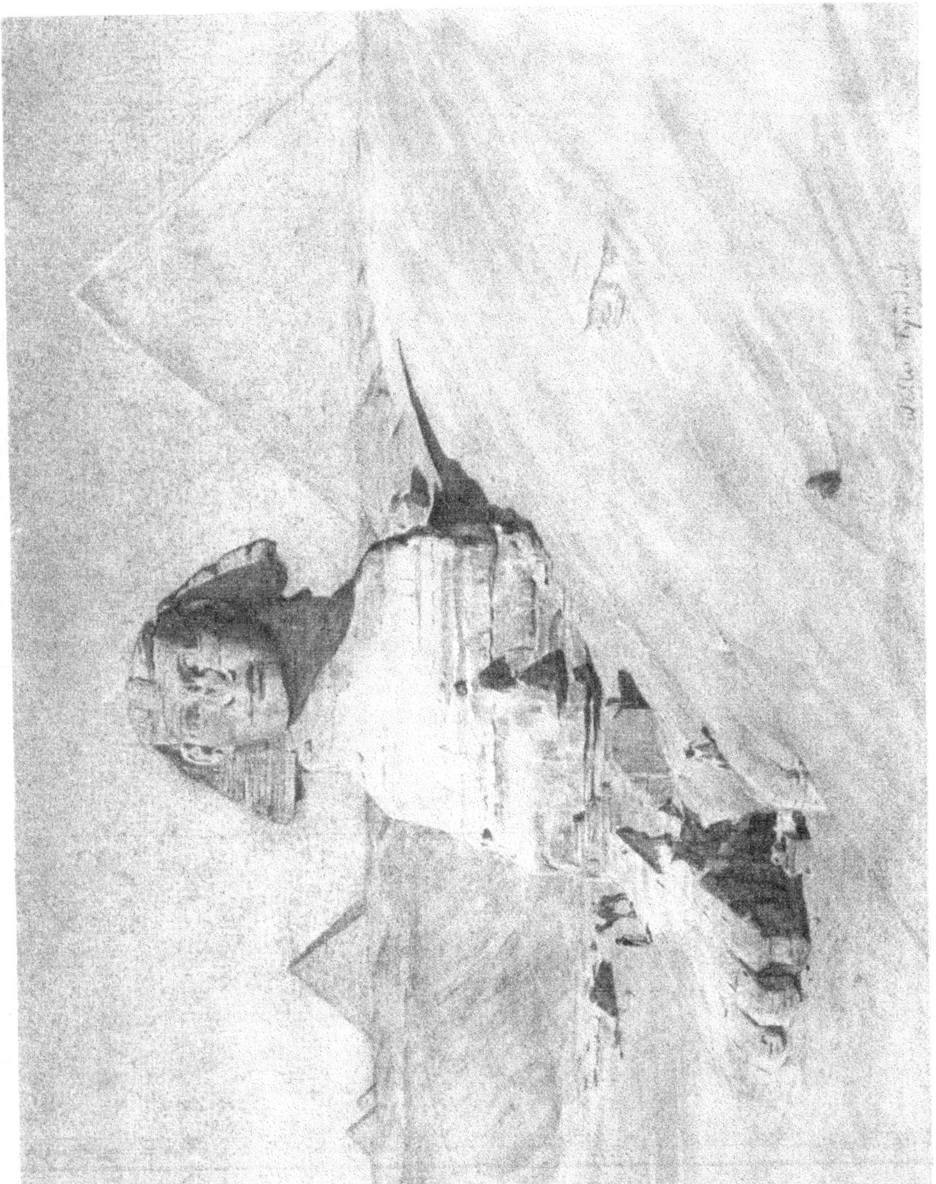

render that imperturbable expression which Egypt's greatest artists could give to the presentments of their gods and their Pharaohs. Who this Pharaoh was is still a point that Egyptologists differ about. The sculptor who hewed the features out of this rock doubtless sought more to present an embodiment of kingship than an exact likeness of the Pharaoh who set him his task.

In spite of any prejudice which we may have to an organised outing with the moon thrown in as a theatrical property, it is advisable to take an opportunity of seeing the Sphinx by the light of the full moon. It is ten years since the writer saw it under those conditions, but it was so impressive a sight that he yet hopes to be able to record it from recollection.

No one can have spent much time within sketching distance of the Sphinx without being struck by the ever-recurring remarks of the numerous people who come to see it. One question that I have heard asked in many languages sticks to my memory more than any other,—"What is he thinking about?" The answer by an Irish priest to whom I heard this query addressed is worth recording: "He is thinking how much butter might be churned out of the milk of human kindness." It was spoken with a certain tone of conviction that silenced laughter, and the rest of the party forbore to try and solve the riddle of the Sphinx until the good padre had left them. A powerful effort not to yell with laughter was required on another occasion. This delightful old priest had designed a treat for some members of his flock in Old Ireland, and this was to send them a photograph of himself, dressed as an Arab Sheykh, sitting on the hump of a camel, gazing away to the far horizon, with the Sphinx and the pyramids looming up in the background. His shaven jowl looked comical enough under the turban, and the thin, pale extremities visible beneath the folds of the "burnous" reminded me of the cockneys that one may see paddling on Margate sands on a bank holiday. However, he seemed pleased, and no doubt his flock in Ireland would be pleased also; all might have been well but that there remained the camel to reckon with. The beast did not seem inclined to rise upon its legs and needed a good deal of persuasion; the peculiar growl they give when they fight shy of their burden seemed on this occasion to suggest that he did not see the joke. Donkey boys, who are ever ready to use their sticks, now assisted the drivers, and in response to their protests, the hind quarters of the ungainly brute rose suddenly, jerking the Irishman forward, then up went its neck, before our friend had righted himself, causing the heads of the ridden and the rider to come into violent contact, and a bleeding nose and a rapidly swelling eye showed that the poor priest was a good deal hurt. It is fortunate that his flock did not hear his powerful language ; but, addressed as it was to a camel unaccustomed to the Hibernian accent, the words fell on deaf ears, and the brute's expression was as immovable as that of the Sphinx. I was not privileged to see the photograph, and though I saw a good deal of the padre afterwards, and can remember that eye going through all the colours of my palette, we somehow avoided the subject of Arab Sheykhs and camels, and only touched lightly on photography.

The excursion from the Gîzeh pyramids to Sakkâra is a delightful one if the previous night has been spent at the Mena House Hotel; but to attempt to combine the two expeditions in one day, starting from Cairo, is to crowd more sights into a short space of time than the mind can appreciate.

The hire of camels can be arranged for at the hotel, also the provisions for a long day's excursion. However much one resents the existence of modernity in the vicinity of these grand old monuments, one speedily forgives that of the Mena House Hotel. Few more delightful places to stay at exist. Away from the noise and the smells of Cairo, yet near enough to be able to spend a day in the town ; the large terrace where one can sit sheltered from cold winds, or shaded from the sun if it is too hot; the unique outlook, and always that exhilarating dry air, combine to make one look back on a sojourn there as one of the happiest memories of a lifetime.

As the crow flies, Sâkkara is twenty miles from Mena House, but a few more may be allowed for the camel's more tortuous flight. Skirting the margin of the desert for an hour or more we pass the pyramids of Zâwiyet on our right, and, continuing our course for a similar time, we reach a whole cluster of pyramids, but, made *blasé* by our acquaintance with those of Cheops and Khephren, we pass these smaller and rather dilapidated structures with an indulgent smile. The character of the landscape on our right is as distinct from that on our left as it is possible to conceive: the glare of the great desert which we are skirting is in striking contrast to the vivid green that covers the plain just below us. The colour is broken here and there by villages and palm groves, and a grey line marks the connecting causeways. The Nile, which courses through this verdant plain some five miles to the east, is bordered on the further side by only a narrow strip of green which is slightly greyed by the moisture rising from the valley. The hills of the Arabian desert, far grander in outline than those which curtail our view of the great Sahara,

form a lovely background. Egypt is indeed "the gift of the river"!

An entirely different race people this area. The *fellah* is as unlike the Bedawi as we are to either. The Beduin, who have made their home round the pyramids for many generations, are despised by their nomadic kin, and though retaining the features and garb of the latter they have lost the qualities that make these people so interesting.

We soon come in sight of the village of Mit Rahîneh, which stands on the site of Memphis, and of the causeway connecting it with Sakkâra—Sakkâra, which has given its name to the necropolis of the ancient capital.

Pitfalls in the sand, silent witnesses of the desecration of the dead, oblige us to pick our way more carefully, and the dark mouths of rock-cut tombs in the low-lying cliffs make us aware that we are entering a vast burial-ground. Potsherds and other débris of the rifled graves are strewn about everywhere, but the brilliancy of the light and the brightness of the dry, sandy soil prevent the gruesome feelings one would experience on entering a plundered cemetery in Europe. The "step pyramid" dominates the scene, and around it are clustered a number of smaller ones.

After lunch at Mariette's House we are taken to the Serapeum. It is not within the scope of this book to enlarge on the archæological interest of these world-famed monuments. The name of Steindorff at the head of the historical notice in your Baedeker is sufficient guarantee that these interests have been well looked after.

How Mariette was led to discover these Apis tombs, from a passage in Strabo, is given by Amelia B. Edwards in her *Thousand Miles Up the Nile*. This author's impressions of her visit to Sakkâra leave little to be said by the writer of this volume, whose recollections of a walk through the dimly lighted vaults containing the sarcophagi of the sacred bulls are all subordinate to the remembrance of feeling nearly stifled and of longing to regain the fresh air outside.

The tomb of Tyi, which marks the first great epoch of pictorial art, enters more within the range of this volume. The low reliefs that cover the walls of this fifth-dynasty sepulchre bear much the same relation to the maturer art of the eighteenth dynasty as that of Cimabue or even Giotto does to that of Raphael. But whereas, in the latter case, these periods are separated by only a century and a half, and we can trace a continuous growth, twelve centuries and more intervene in the former. Neither is the development so continuous in Egyptian art. After reaching this high level in the fifth dynasty it sinks and almost disappears during the following ones ; it rises again towards the eleventh, but seems to be entirely lost during the dark ages of the Hyksos. However, the art of this wonderful race appears to be inextinguishable ; for no sooner have the Thothmes cleared the country of the alien rulers, than it rises once more to the height of what we are now admiring, and surpasses it before Ramses II. makes it subservient to his own personal glorification.

Here, as in the work at Dêr el-Bahri, the fine quality of the limestone allows of most delicate cutting, and the figures in both cases are firmly outlined, but are very slightly relieved from the background. Being highly coloured a high relief would have been superfluous. In spite of the long lapse of time much of the convention of this early work is still visible in Hatshepsu's temple at Dêr el-Bahri, and it is evident that the art of the latter is a development of these mural paintings rather than of the intermediate work of the eleventh dynasty.

Later on we shall have more to say of the eighteenth dynasty work, which, though more subtle, surprises one less than these Tyi reliefs, which are the first manifestations of a living art following a rude convention. A study of these tombs of Sakkâra helps one to appreciate the unique collections in the Cairo Museum, as this necropolis has supplied it with so many of its finest works.

The ride to Bedrashên, where we take the train to Cairo, leads us past the heaps of rubbish that mark the site of Memphis, and the two colossal statues of Ramses II. The villages we pass, with the pylon-shaped columbaria and backing of palm groves, are slightly raised above the level of the plain, looking from a distance like islands on a very emerald sea. At the high Nile they are islands in more than appearance, and there is no mistaking how far the fertilising waters then extend. The flocks and herds driven in from their pasturage, and the many rustic scenes we witness, recall the wall paintings in Tyi's tomb, for which these might have served as models four millenniums and a half ago. Interesting as the landscape is at present, it is far more paintable when these green fields have turned to gold and the harvesting has begun. Improved agricultural implements are not much in evidence, and the work of the *fellah* now is carried on in much the same way as in pharaonic times.

The women, returning from the river carrying pitchers on their heads, are clothed in much the same way as their sisters in the towns, but their faces are unveiled. The more arduous work they

do would make the yashmak quite unbearable, but they turn away their eyes from the "Firangi," or will draw the loose veil that hangs from their heads across their faces—an intimation that their barefacedness is a necessity which the "Firangi" would do well to respect.

The view from the train, over the fifteen miles that take us back to Cairo, is at its best now; the evening light catches Gebel Turra beyond Helwan on the further side of the Nile, and delicate violet shadows in a golden mass of colour give the drawing of the rock strata. The villages on our left are silhouetted against the shades of the Libyan desert and the palm groves stand out in bold masses against the sunset sky. As we near Cairo the line runs for a while near the river's edge; the light now turning to pink catches the sails of the "gyassas" and is repeated in a lower tone on the Mokattam hills in the distance. Near Gîzeh the twilight lends a mystery to the groups of figures on the Nile bank and the sails of the boats, until, grey against the afterglow reflected on the hills, the little town itself, which is not particularly interesting in broad daylight, suggests all sorts of possibilities in the increasing darkness. In due course we reach gaslit Cairo, feeling grateful for the beautiful evening that has ended so interesting a day.

CHAPTER XI

Alexandria to Cairo

I left Egypt shortly after my last visit to Sakkâra, and during the eight following winters I was working under European skies. I often longed to return to the sunshine and dry atmosphere of the Nile valley ; and while shivering at my work in some Italian town, or seeking shelter from the rain in England or France, that delightful excursion to Sakkâra would return to my mind. A commission to make a series of water-colour drawings of Egypt brought these longings to a happy issue. I returned *via* Alexandria after a sufficient period had elapsed to make me able to feel something of the delight, if not of the excitement, that a first visit gives.

The journey to Cairo by this route gives one a different impression of the country than the one taken *via* Port Said. In neither of the ports does one get that foretaste of the East that one gets on

landing at many a place on the African coast which may be considerably west of Greenwich. Your map proves to you that you are in Egypt, but there is little in either town to make you realise that "Land of Egypt," associated from earliest childhood with Pharaohs (hard-hearted or otherwise) and the children of Israel. Both places are more suited to give an Egyptian who is leaving his country a foretaste of Europe. It is on the two roads to Cairo that the impressions of the country are of so different a nature.

I have endeavoured before to give some idea of the route from Port Said; it may be of interest to follow me in this run through the Delta before we can proceed to Upper Egypt.

The first half-hour takes you through some prosperous-looking suburbs, built at considerable cost with a minimum amount of architectural taste. The want of shade, and possibly the wish to hide structural deficiencies, has fortunately induced the occupiers to devote a good deal of care to their gardens. In spite of the hungry-looking soil, beautiful trees and flowering shrubs do their best to screen and to make attractive the sorry sight which most of these houses are when they first leave the builder's hands.

The train skirts the coast for a few miles, and no sooner has it curved round the northern edge of the Lake of Maryût, and begun to cross the rich alluvial soil of the Delta, than the whole landscape is changed. Villadom comes to an abrupt end; the trowsered oriental with his 'tarboush' gives way to the robed and turbaned *fellah;* the motor-car can go no further, and is replaced by the camel or the ass. The villages that are dotted all over the landscape, as is the case on very productive soils, must look much the same now as they looked to the children of Israel, when they were less profitably engaged than at present, in the service of the Pharaohs. The houses then, as now, were built of mud bricks, and covered with a similar thatch, or roofed with transversely laid palm trunks with mud trodden into the interstices, and the dome may also have been there, as we find that form of roofing in dynastic times. Each successive invader adapted himself to what he found, as being most suitable to the soil he had acquired, and though the worship of Isis gave way to that of the risen Christ, and Islam has since held sway, the appearance of the landscape has altered less in four millenniums than that of an English county has done in four centuries. No dense forests had to be cleared, as with us, before the deep alluvial deposits which form the Delta brought forth corn. It is true that corn is not the main crop now, but cotton; but, in the general aspect of a landscape, a crop is a crop, green in its youth and mellow in its age.

The minaret that bespeaks a changed faith is seldom seen, which is accounted for by the dearness of all building material except mud. A square enclosure, built of sun-dried bricks with some rude Arab decoration round the door, serves as the village mosque. The tops of the chimneyless houses have their flat outline broken by layers of produce placed there to dry, and often by broken pitchers, which serve as nesting places for doves. The peasants and their cattle live in close proximity, and the head of a camel may be seen peering out of a half-opened door. Increased irrigation has extended the area of cultivation, and much marshy land has been drained; but, on the whole, what now meets the eye of the tourist, as the Cairo express hurries him along to Shepheard's or the Savoy, is very similar to what met that of Joseph when he went his rounds in Pharaoh's service. To the east, right away to the horizon, stretches this tract of rich land, where the villages appear to touch each other, then slowly to separate, and become blotted out, one by one, by a nearer clump of palms. The squeal of a "sakiyeh" is just discernible above the rattle of the train; it gets louder; a tableau of an archaic waterwheel worked by a buffalo glides across the foreground and, before the creaky noise has died away, you are brought back to the twentieth century by an oriental—Europeanised up to his neck—who wants to clip your ticket.

So far we have no sight of Father Nile, though signs of his gifts stretch from horizon to horizon; but we have had glimpses of the Mahmûdîeh canal, the great work of Mohammed Ali, which revived the prosperity of Alexandria by connecting that city with the great waterway of Egypt, and now and again the rich colour of the soil has been emphasised by the reflection of the sky upon one of the lesser canals that vein the map of the Delta. When the train slows down to halt at Kafr ez-Zaiyât, the Rosetta branch of the Nile is before us, and as we cross the bridge we catch sight of boats being laden with the products of this rich country, or discharging earthenware pitchers and sugar-cane from Upper Egypt, or cases and machinery bearing the mark of some English firm. A group of corrugated iron sheds and chimneys recall some of the ugliness we hoped to have left behind us when leaving the last European port, but the glorious light that envelops everything prevents even these from jarring too much with the picturesqueness of the Nile bank.

A short run from here and we reach Tanta, a flourishing town lying midway between the two

W. Tyndale

arms of the river, which has separated at the Barrage near Cairo. The saint Seyid el-Bedawi is buried here; his shrine is not worth a visit for its architectural beauty, but it must be a most interesting sight to see the thousands of pilgrims, from every part of the Mohammedan world, who flock here on "Môlid"—the day of his birth. This unfortunately takes place in August; but, in spite of the heat, the writer still hopes some day to witness this fair and view the half million of pilgrims that congregate there upon that anniversary.

Leaving Tanta the train runs through the fattest land of this fertile plain, the fatness of which is evidenced by the cotton-cleaning mills, which do not improve the landscape. We cross the eastern arm of the Nile on reaching Bulâk, and from this place to Cairo we traverse the same country to which we have referred in an earlier part of this book.

Perhaps it is my love of Egypt and things Egyptian that makes me dislike Cairo, or, I should say, the European quarter in which one is compelled to live. Leaving Europe when the chill and frequent rain of October makes one thankful to avoid a long winter, the joy of being once more under a blue sky, with the prospect of months of outdoor work, instead of the confinement to a studio, should all tend to prejudice one in favour of this city ; but, unhappily, the Cairo one lives in is not the beautiful old town one has come to paint. They lie side by side, but have little in common save the sky that covers them both. Accommodation is not to be had in the old quarters, or little of the new would ever trouble me. The people have as alien an appearance as the houses they live in ; to make their fortunes as rapidly as they can out of the natives or the winter visitors, and then to retire to their own countries is, of course, the *raison d'être* of their presence, but this bit of modern Europe harmonises badly with its neighbour, the picturesque mediæval city.

Before the Hôtel du Nil closed its doors it was possible to live in the midst of the surroundings one had come so far to paint ; but the artist now must live in the modern quarter, and the spirit of that quarter (to make all one can and as quickly as one can) is very liable to have a bad effect on his art. If you stop at a modest inn where few of the British colony would deign to call, it is irritating to be charged much the same as at a first-rate hotel on the Riviera; but put up at one of those huge caravanserais that cater for *la haute société*, and you are charged exorbitantly for the privilege of using rooms where a show of costliness does not console you for the poor design and colour of the decoration and furniture. Some units of this *haute societe* are no more to your liking than the pretentious apartments, and visits from those who ignored your existence when lodging in humbler quarters can easily be dispensed with. Most of one's day is spent in the more congenial surroundings of the old city; but to eat, drink, or sleep, one must return to these less congenial quarters. One recalls with regret the simple inns in Italy, where, if the fare was modest, the reckoning was still more so, and the kindly welcome of the padrone made one forget both.

It is perhaps unreasonable to expect things to be different, and for a short stay it does not matter, but if one is sojourning for some time, number so-and-so, whose spending capacities are all that interest the host, is liable to suffer from home sickness. However, during the last two years I have fortunately been able to do my work in more congenial surroundings. The dahabiyeh, the tent, and the excavator's camp have been all much more to my liking.

Life on a dahabiyeh, as the house-boat of the Nile is called, is as near an ideal state of existence as an artist can find on this earth. There are but few places in Egypt that cannot be reached by these boats; and to have a home on board one of these, with sympathetic companionship, a studio, and a dependable climate, near a chosen sketching ground, gives him a chance of doing the very best that he is capable of.

A tent, with a trusty servant to fend for one's wants, is perhaps the next best thing, and is within the reach of a larger number, but there is some difficulty in finding a suitable place to pitch it. The land round most of the ancient monuments has been acquired by the Antiquities Department, which will allow no stranger to camp there. As the ground is for the most part desert, this may savour of the dog in the manger, but it is a necessary restriction. Before this ground was acquired, people would often camp within easy reach of the excavations, and the temptations to acquire portable antiquities, which belong to the Department, were often too strong to resist. An Arab offers to sell some scarabs or a blue glazed 'ushabti'; the question the visitor usually asks himself is whether they are genuine; he does not as a rule concern himself as to whether it is stolen property or not. If the Arab is sure that the new comer is in no way connected with the excavations, he will even admit the theft, as a proof that the objects are not frauds. It is sufficiently difficult for the Department to check the thieving of the workmen in its employ, and it is therefore too much to expect it to encourage the advent of neighbours who so readily receive these goods.

This necessary restriction is hard upon those whose only object is to camp near the subjects they wish to paint; but, as Professor Maspero, the distinguished head of the Department, explained to me, it was impossible to avoid making a hard and fast rule, and that, as guardians for the country of these treasures, they could not allow anything which might endanger their safety. Wherever he is able to assist the student without risk to his trust, he is always most obliging, and the Inspectors of Antiquities, who have the guardianship of the four districts under him, are equally courteous and helpful to anyone seriously wishing to study or to paint any of the monuments.

It so happened that a concession was granted to the Metropolitan Museum of New York to take impressions of a portion of the bas reliefs in Hatshepsu's temple at Thebes. The casts from these, after being coloured as much like the original wall as possible, are to be set up in this museum, which will give the New Yorkers an opportunity of studying the most delightful bit of wall decoration of the eighteenth dynasty. Mr. Laffan, who is generously defraying the expense, deputed Mr. Currelly, who was at the time in charge of the excavations, to see the work carried out, and to find an artist to do the colouring. This work was offered to me, and, with the proviso that I should be allowed to devote half my days to my water colours, I accepted it.

My stay in Cairo was a short one; for being asked by Erskine Nicol to stay on his dahabiyeh, then lying at Boulâk, I was only a couple of days at an hotel, and the *Mavis* formed the base of my operations until the camp at Thebes was in readiness for the winter's work. The boat was undergoing some repairs, but my host, a brother brush, being as little in sympathy as myself with *la haute société* and the hotel life of Cairo, judged that I would prefer to put up with the smell of paint and the inevitable disorder rather than stay on where I was.

Parts of Boulâk are still unspoilt, and the fruit stalls and pot market are as delightful as they ever were. Whether this is less painted than other parts of the town, or whether the inhabitants suffer from a double dose of original curiosity, I cannot say, but a more inquisitive lot I never worked amongst. My faithful Mohammed was unable to be with me or possibly I might have been less bothered. A word from him to a policeman, and an invented relationship of the "hawaga" to some powerful "Moufetish," might have cleared the street of the curious and it would then only have been necessary to indemnify the holder of the stall or shop for the possible customer he might have lost. To

retire to the dahabiyeh, after the noise, heat, flies and all other unpleasantnesses which the close proximity of these people entails, is a joy indeed. The clang and clamour of the works near us had ceased, and no sound but the occasional plashing of an oar would disturb us while enjoying a peaceful cigarette and watching the sunset from the deck.

To sail up to Thebes on my friend's dahabiyeh was a pleasure time would not permit me to enjoy. I had spent some weeks on the *Mavis* in the previous spring, when we were drifting down the river, and I appreciated what I was losing in not being able to accept my friend's invitation. The prospects of rejoining him at Karnak, when the season's work at Dêr el-Bahri would be ended, somewhat consoled me. A night's journey in the Luxor train is a much more prosaic mode of progression, but the two or three weeks' time needed to sail that distance was out of the question.

CHAPTER XII

Thebes

I ARRIVED at Luxor on the first of December; and the train being only a matter of four hours late did not seem to surprise those who had come to meet me, any more than it surprised the camel which had also been waiting that time, on the Thebes side of the Nile, to take my luggage to the camp. A queer load did the beast carry that afternoon! Paints in one pannier would be counterbalanced by pickles and tins in the other, a sack of plaster of Paris weighing more than a portmanteau, with sardines and candles stuffed round it to equalise matters. And, ye gods! what a lot of sardines! The delicious savoury that looks so well on a background of toast; would it look equally well served up in platefuls as a *pièce de résistance?* Were those other tins also filled with the delectable little fish? No, their place of origin, the revelations concerning which have lately made many a cheek turn pale, at least reassured me that I was not to undergo a strict sardine cure. Some bags of flour that were being balanced against my sketching apparatus reassured me yet more. When the easel had been well wedged in one pannier and the sketching umbrella in the other, Mohammed Effendi, who represented the Egyptian Exploration Fund, gave the orders to march. He and I mounted our donkeys and the "commissaree camuel" followed in our rear.

The donkey as we know it in England is a sorry kind of mount, and no one but a circus clown would dare turn up at a meet upon such a steed; but when British sporting enterprise has introduced packs of hounds into the country, the Egyptian donkey will figure largely in the field.

A half mile of sand and dried mud separated the river from the cultivated land, and a brisk canter across this left the camel and its driver well behind. After passing some enclosed gardens, and crossing the canal bridge, we descended into the wide green plain separating the necropolis of Thebes from the river. The colossi of Amenhotep III. stand on the further end of the cultivation, and upon the left of them, on the edge of the desert, we can just discern the pylons of the great temple of Medînet Habu. The ruins of the Ramesseum are partly hidden by trees, and the amphitheatre formed by the cliffs that back the temple of Dêr el-Bahri is just visible beyond. A couple of miles' ride and we leave the colossi on our left, but we can still see the darkened bases that show the reach of the waters during the yearly inundations of the Nile. We pass alongside the broken pylon of the Ramesseum which stands just above the cultivated plain that we are now leaving. Here we have to pick our way through open tombs and the pile of débris that has been thrown out at different periods. Tombs are now the main feature of the whole landscape before us; often pits and low rubbish hills break up the surface of the ground, until it reaches an outlying part of the village of Kurnah, which stands on a higher level.

We ascend between the huts of the village, and some half naked little urchins, rolling in the dust, or running after some hungry-looking fowls, are a welcome sign of life in this vast cemetery. From a larger hollow than most of those which we have passed, a woman's shrill voice calls out to the children to leave the chickens alone. Looking down, one realises that this hollow is but the entrance to one or more burial-places, and the square black hole into which the woman disappears, and which is now the doorway of her dwelling, is the open mouth of a tomb. One or two square, mud-brick houses are the residences of the more well-to-do; the rest of the population

of this scattered and extensive village either live entirely in tombs, or use tombs as a part of their dwelling.

A low mud wall surrounds part of a court to prevent persons or animals from tumbling into the enclosure, and curious erections, like gigantic toadstools with their edges curved upwards, rise from the floor. They are built of sun-dried mud, are rudely ornamented, and are of various heights. Some of these were filled with straw or fodder, but they are not constructed for this purpose, though they are useful in the winter to store things out of reach of the goats. It is as an out-door resting place that these are really built, and their peculiar shape is well adapted to prevent scorpions from becoming bed-fellows. On the outside edge of the hollow, where the sleeper lies curled up at night, are one or two projections shaped like egg-cups, which are large enough to hold a "kulla," the porous earthen water-bottle. It is, perhaps, fortunate that scorpions have made these folk abandon the close sepulchre for so airy a resting-place. What cooking is done takes place inside the habitation, and the smoke has no other outlet than the entrance. Some of the more fortunate inhabitants have several of these rock-cut tombs opening on to the courtyard, in which case one serves as a sleeping apartment during the winter season, when the scorpions are hibernating, another as kitchen, and the others house such live-stock as the owner possesses. The dwellings vary a good deal according to the position of the tomb which forms the nucleus. This is, in places, some feet up the side of a cliff, when a square-roofed hut is built against it, enclosing the entrance, and the tomb itself serves as a second apartment, having a few stone steps leading into it.

Descending the ridge of land near these dwellings, one observes the entrances to sepulchres with closed iron doors, with the slopes down to them cleared of débris and an official number on each lintel. They are less picturesque externally than those that we have passed, but they evidently possess something of importance. These are some of the tombs of the Sheykh Abd el-Kurnah ; but we shall have occasion to speak of them later on, so at present we continue our road.

A ruined mud-brick tower, with some walls above, suggests the remains of an early Coptic convent ; but I am informed that they date no further back than the early part of the last century and are the remains of the house in which Wilkinson lived. Here he collected most of the material for his "Manners and Customs of the Ancient Egyptians,"—a book considered out of date by some, but which is most interesting reading, and is illustrated with great knowledge by the author. He died, I am told, by a gun accident, in this house where he had spent so much of his time. When the poor man was dying, a fear that suspicion might fall upon his servants caused him to send for the "Omdeh" or chief of the village, and he made a declaration that his carelessness alone had caused the accident, and that no one but himself was to blame. This probably saved the necks of his servants, for in those days a suspicion was often enough fatal to those upon whom it fell, especially if a foreign Government pressed for an inquiry.

We now enter the huge amphitheatre formed by the limestone cliffs that circle round the western end of the Dêr el-Bahri valley. The terraced and colonnaded temple of Hatshepsu stands at the base, and faces the temple of Luxor some four miles away, upon the other side of the Nile. It would have been hard to find a finer site, or a more imposing background than this. A low stone hut nearer to us, and to the left of the temple, is at this moment interesting me more than anything else; for this hut is to be my home for the next five months. The dust arising from the foundations of an earlier temple to the left of that of Hatshepsu showed that the excavations were in full swing, and we could hear the sing-song of the crowd of workmen on the dig.

My friend Currelly was up at the excavations, but a cheery welcome from an American who was in charge of the hut soon made me feel at home. Three young Arabs, who were cook, butler and footman respectively, kissed my hand, tendered their greetings, and then composed themselves for a long stare.

Mr. Dennis, who was acting host, sent off Albrikman, the cook, to prepare tea, and Bulbul, the waiter, fished out a cloth and spread it over a packing case, or table, I should say, to give it its future dignity. The third Arab youth, Achmet, continued his stare; he had, so far, only thoroughly contemplated my hat, and there yet remained a good hour's staring before he would reach my boots; but he had hardly got as far as my shoulders, when an unnecessary craving on my part for a wash obliged him to defer taking me thoroughly in till a more convenient period. I gathered that as we had parted company with the "commissaree camuel" at the river's edge, my luggage might be expected to arrive in an hour. I had been able to complete my toilet in a tent near the hut, when a long whistle, and a shout from what appeared an army of workmen, apprised me that the day's work was over. This shouting, which seemed to come from every part of the valley, gave me the impression that very extensive excavations must be going on. One of the camp dogs then started barking,

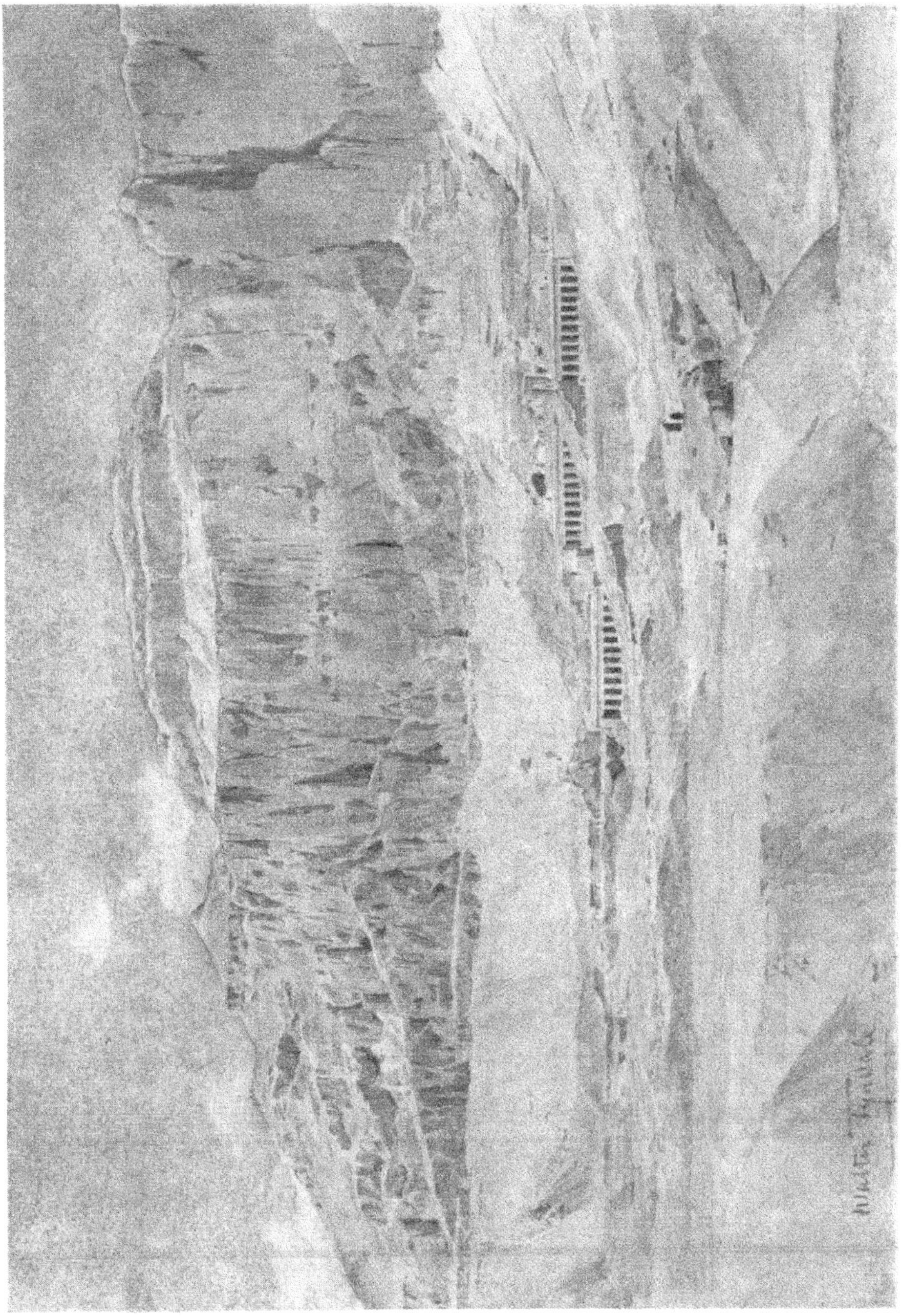

and the sound was repeated again and again, as if all the curs of the surrounding country were responding. Sticking my head out of the tent to call for a towel—"towel, towel, towel!" my voice returned in a diminuendo, till it died away in the distance. This repeating echo added to the weirdness of my new quarters.

The sun had sunk behind the western cliffs which enclose the valley, and its rays were only reflected on the heights to the east; the hollow which, in the full light, was broken by shapeless heaps of débris, reminding one unpleasantly of London when the streets are up, was now glorified by a luminous shadow, warm in the near foreground and deepening its violet hue till it met the rich gold above. Tea, the increasing beauty of the valley as well as the cessation of noise, put me in the best of humours. We were ioined by a second member of the dig, a Major Griffith, and presently Currelly returned from the works and joined our tea party. There was much to talk about. The casting of the expedition to Punt, which I had hoped was well started, had not begun. The two natives who had had some slight experience in that kind of work had been bribed away to another dig, and it seemed doubtful when I should be able to commence my part of the work. Ways and means were discussed long after the valley was in complete darkness, with not a light to be seen but that of the candles on our improvised tea table.

The camel at last turned up, and I began to consider arrangements for the night. There were two empty rooms leading out of a general sitting-room in the hut, and a large store-room for the "finds," from which a faint smell of mouse and mummy proceeded. The two former chambers, were, however, to be occupied by two lady visitors who were expected from Cairo the next day, and I was still in doubt as to what were to be my quarters for the next few months. Where was I to sleep; and upon what? I was beginning to think that even the much-despised luxurious hotel in Cairo; "replete with every modern comfort," was not such a bad thing after all. However, Bulbul produced a native bedstead, which he placed in an open space between heaps of broken stones that had been brought down from the excavations, Achmet followed with a mattress, and my bedroom was complete. It was spacious, for it embraced the whole valley with the star-spangled firmament for the ceiling. It took a good deal of lighting, for the wind, which generally rises an hour after sunset, had not forgotten us that night, and made short work of the candles. My friend seemed surprised that I could not see to pick my way in the dark through the broken bits of temple that lay everywhere. I assured him that many of my countrymen suffered from the same complaint, and he humanely led me back to the hut. A tent near our two beds (I had not noticed the second couch till I stumbled over it in the dark) served as a dressing-room for both of us. My friend is a Canadian, and has had much experience in camping out, both in his own country and in Egypt; he must have smiled as he heard the "tenderfoot" trip up over the tent ropes. Darkness hid the smile, though I fancied I heard it; a novel situation is liable to make one fanciful! A remaining quarter of the moon was to appear later on, so I postponed further bedroom arrangements and let my baggage lie where the camel had left it.

The sitting-room of the hut seemed a blaze of light when we reached it; the table was set, and I was awaiting an enormous dish of sardines; as I had imagined that this with pickles was an excavator's sole diet, and was what I had been prepared to expect from the load of the camel. Bulbul appeared very soon with a steaming bowl of soup, to be repulsed by Achmet, who, with the help of Dennis, was preparing a *hors-d'œuvre*. Sardines, I thought; but no, a dish of delicious little anchovies, fresh from a swim in their native oil and resting amongst some stoned olives, were presently brought in. Standing at the head of the table, the dish carried true waiter fashion, ear high, on back-stretched hand, Achmet solemnly announced that dinner was served. A popping of corks came from the direction of Bulbul, who, as a true son of Egypt, bore little resentment for his previous rebuff. The soup was none the worse when it appeared a second time, and the whole of the dinner was eaten with that best of sauces,—the sharp appetite produced by the crisp desert air.

The varied experiences of the four who made up the party supplied plenty of subject for conversation. The Major had served two years in South Africa during the Boer War; Currelly had had a long experience in excavating, and had spent a season with Flinders Petrie exploring the Sinaitic peninsula; Dennis, who hails from the southern States, had a fund of anecdotes which he could shoot in whenever there was a gap in the flow of talk, and I even was fortunate enough to get a story well landed. Early hours obtain in the camp, and the half moon having kept its appointment, I was able to ferret out a heavy rug from my baggage, and to reach my bed without barking my shins.

Now sleeping in the open with comfort is not learnt in one night in the desert any more than elsewhere. The valley which we were in still retained some of the heat of a long day's sun, and

my bed was at first uncomfortably warm. The wind had dropped, so I anticipated no trouble from that quarter, but the barking of a dog, that some well directed stones failed to silence, promised badly. This, however, was a minor discomfort compared with the wind and the cold later on. Currelly had slept out so often, and was so sound a sleeper, that he could have slumbered on a toasting-fork. Two guards were there and it was their business to wake up, each time the brutes barked, to see if anyone was about. I was quite willing to leave all the waking up to them, but I could not help sharing in it myself.

At first I rather enjoyed lying awake; there was a pleasure in the novelty, and the moonlight on the cliffs made them appear even grander than when I saw them by daylight. The air was deliciously fresh, and the Arab blanket that I had bought in the Tunis bazaar kept me beautifully warm. The dogs had been silent for some time, and I was becoming pleasantly conscious of consciousness departing, when a howl from a jackal started the two brutes barking again. Shades of Thebes, what a noise they made! One started off like a flash in the direction of the howl, which I counted a mercy, while the second one contented itself by barking nearer home; and not only did the echoes take up the noise, but the dog of the guards at the Hatshepsu temple joined in. The moon had sunk behind the cliffs, so I must really have slept some time ; it was very nearly dark, but I could see an object lying where the loudest bark came from, and, feeling about for a stone, I lit on a bit of Currelly's palæolithic collection and let fly at the dark object. I hit it, but it proved to be an empty petroleum tin, and not my enemy. The noise seemed to wake no one else ; happy people ! I got into bed again and soon fell fast asleep. I dreamt that the noise was awakening the dead, and that mummies were creeping out of every pit I had passed on my way here. Then I felt like a mummy myself, and dreamed that the tombstone which covered me was making attempts to raise itself. A cold shiver ran through me at each of its efforts. A sensation of lightness as though the stone had lifted entirely, and the frenzied dance of an empty petroleum tin which appeared to be making merry awoke me completely. A howling wind had risen, and my heavy Tunis blanket had disappeared in the darkness. I tumbled about the stones in search of it and bumped up against a man. This proved to be one of the guards who had come to my assistance, and who found the blanket. He spread this over the bed so that a piece overlapped and rested upon the ground on each side. Half an Osiride figure was lifted on to one piece while I stood on the other to keep it in place. I could not face the wind for the dust, and my ears and neck smarted from the particles that were blown against them. Fragments of temple were now placed on the portion of the blanket upon which I had been standing, and I found my way to the dressing-tent to put my clothes on, as I was now bitterly cold in nothing but pyjamas. How this tent stood against the wind was a marvel. Hearing the major's voice I peeped out and found he was struggling to disengage himself from his canvas, which had been blown down. The striking of matches in the next tent, which was still standing, showed that the wind was too much for Dennis, and that he was preparing to spend the night in the hut in preference to being enveloped in his. The guard shouting to his mate to come and help woke Currelly, and the boys arrived with lanterns. They managed to extract the mattresses from the tents, and Griffith and Dennis slept indoors, while Currelly and I decided to see the night out where we were, and, tying handkerchiefs over our faces to keep the dust out, we got into bed again. I was thankful to have got into my clothes, for my wonderful blanket of which I had boasted was not enough of itself to keep out the increasing cold. The wind that had awakened us all seemed now to help to lull us to sleep, and I knew no more of the storm that night.

The sun rising above the hills beyond Luxor woke me up, and in spite of a disturbed night, I felt very much refreshed ; for which the absence of stuffiness in my vast dormitory may have accounted. The wind had completely dropped, and not a sound but some heavy breathing near me could I hear. How seldom does one enjoy the beauty of sunrise while leading a life in town. My stay in this camp gave me plenty of opportunity to do so, as the approaching light never failed to awaken me. This was very well during the winter months, for the sun then rises only some forty minutes earlier than in England, but when the days lengthened out in the spring, I did not appreciate being awakened so very long before there was any chance of breakfast.

Groups of workmen soon appeared, filing along the entrance to the valley, looking like little black silhouettes against the misty light in the east. At seven o'clock some 300 men and boys were grouped near the camp, while Mohammed Effendi called the roll. I was now able to see to open my baggage and to arrange what I wanted in the dressing tent, but my heart sank when I gathered from one of the Arab servants that breakfast was not till eight o'clock, for this open-air treatment made me feel a sinking in another part of my anatomy. I could have embraced Bulbul when, anticipating my

desires, he brought me a cup of tea. This name of "Bulbul" was one which I had never heard before, so I questioned the lad about it. I found that it was not the name given to him at his birth, but was that of "a bird that sings very well"—(the nightingale, I found out afterwards). He modestly admitted that it was his voice which had earned him this nickname, and that he was in great request when the village "Molid" was on.

CHAPTER XIII

THE TEMPLE OF AMMON

AFTER breakfast I took a stroll up to the Hatshepsu temple with Currelly, to study the best means to adopt in order to make the casting with the least risk to the wall painting. We took from the works a couple of men who my friend knew to be adepts at making sham 'antikas,' with some sheets of tin-foil and a lump of wax. Choosing a simple bas-relief to experiment upon, we held the tinfoil against the stone and rubbed it into the cutting with a rag until the impression of the relief began to show clearly upon the surface. The deeper cuttings had then to be pressed in with a stiff hogshair brush. The beeswax, which we placed in the sun to soften, was then pressed upon the tin-foil, and when that was completely covered, care being taken not to let the wax touch any of the wall itself,—we had to wait until the cold surface of the stone had hardened the wax.

The next thing was to take the foil and wax

backing off the stone and lay it face upwards on a flat board. This silvery mould of the bas-relief looked all right to our inexperienced eyes, and the "Quies keteer" of the 'antika' forgers was encouraging. The mould was taken down to the hut, and after giving it a wipe over with grease we took a plaster cast from it.

We then left the plaster to harden, and went to see what was doing in the cloud of dust that was arising from the excavations to the left of the Hatshepsu temple.

The Egyptian Exploration Fund obtained the concession to excavate this early temple in 1903, after the work on its later neighbour had been handed over to the Antiquities Department. Professor Naville gave his services, and, assisted by Henry Hall of the British Museum and latterly by C. T. Currelly, he completed the work in three years. As we ascend the three terraces we notice the similarity of plan to the sanctuary Hatshepsu erected some seven centuries later. There is, however, one feature which distinguishes the temple of Mentuhotep II. from any other, and that is the ruin of a pyramid on the third terrace. It is the only known instance of a pyramid forming an actual part of a temple, and the singularity of this has led to some interesting results. A papyrus in the Turin Museum states that the Pharaoh (one of the later Ramses) appointed a commission to visit the tombs of his predecessors and report upon their condition. In their report they mentioned that the tomb of Mentuhotep II. was intact, but they did not say where this tomb was situated, but a drawing of a pyramid followed the brief allusion to it. This decided Professor Naville to search for this tomb under the pyramid. It was not found, but his labour was rewarded by finding six diorite statues of Usertesen III., three of which are now in the British Museum, and three at Cairo. As this monarch belongs to a later dynasty, namely the XII, it adds one more problem to the many that this temple leaves unsolved.

A pit tomb that was unearthed a few yards behind the base of this pyramid proved to be that of a woman, and some well preserved, though rude, wall paintings of the XI dynasty, which covered the exterior of this sepulchre, were also well worth finding; but where the remains of Mentuhotep lay was still a mystery.

The excavations were carried further into the base of the cliffs that back the temple; the débris from the limestone rocks was cleared, the underlying strata of shale was reached, and great was the surprise of Mr. Dalison, who was at the time directing the workmen, when, without any warning, a mass of broken stone slid down, exposing a deep recess in the rock and the head and shoulders of a Hathor cow. The winter of 1906 was a season of surprises at Thebes, but the suddenness of this one, the beauty of the sculpture, and the perfection of its preservation marked this as an epoch-making find. Currelly, who was on the spot before the dust had subsided, supplied me with the details.

The work had to be carried on with great caution. The native workmen are keenly interested when some valuable object is found, and easily lose their heads when excited. Working into the sides of these cliffs might, if not carried on with great care, cause a land-slip that might have fatal results; therefore some of the rock has to be shorn up before one dare risk dislodging the underlying stone. The nature of the hollow from which this startling head appeared wanted careful study. When the fallen débris was cleared, this hollow proved to be soundly arched; and fairly well preserved wall paintings, that covered the interior, left no doubt as to the period of its construction and that of the magnificent cow which it enshrined. It is regrettable that the whole could not have remained *in situ*. The museum authorities at Cairo, however, naturally anxious to add so fine a specimen of XVIII dynasty sculpture to their collection, made the most of the danger it would run of being damaged in this out of the way locality. The local Inspector of Antiquities, Mr.

Weigall, was, much to his credit, equally keen on its remaining in its proper surroundings, and was willing to hold himself responsible for its keeping. Its impressiveness would have been slightly impaired by the iron gates necessary to prevent it from wanton mischief, or from thieves carrying it away in fragments on the chance of selling them to relic hunters ; but, standing in this niche, in the base of these imposing cliffs, near Hatshepsu's sanctuary, to which it belongs, it would have been a far more impressive sight than it is where it now stands in the Cairo museum. The lining of the shrine has also been set up in the same museum, but the unfortunate resemblance which it now bears to a large dog kennel is bound to strike every one.

The accompanying illustration gives the upper terrace of Mentuhotep's temple, with the ruined base of the pyramid to the right. The southern end of the later temple is in the middle distance, and the cliffs that enclose the valley form the background. In the second hollow to the left is the spot where the Hathor cow was found, but, though well within the area of Mentuhotep's sanctuary, it had no connection with it save that of locality. It was an outlying shrine of the marvellous temple which Queen Hatshepsu erected after the one we are now on had fallen into ruin ; and there are evidences that both had been restored

Walter Tyndale

at a still later date by Ramses II. The hollow to the extreme left of the illustration is where lay the centre of interest of this winter's dig. The mouth of an important tomb had been found, and the arrival of Professor Naville was awaited before actually opening what could easily have proved to be the chief object of his search,—the missing tomb.

Returning to the hut, where the cast had had ample time to set, we proceeded to detach it from the wax that formed the matrix. An impression of the original was there, but the tinfoil necessary to prevent the wax from touching the colour on the wall, had very much rounded the edges of the sharp cutting which gives the original work its vitality. The wax had not reached the full depth of the hollows and a good deal of tooling on the cast would be necessary to give it the sharpness required. Another difficulty presented itself; the wax, that had stiffened sufficiently while on the cold surface of the wall, had softened a good deal before the plaster had been poured over it, and it had sunk slightly where the surface of the backing was not flush with the board it was laid on.

Before attempting the next stone, we procured an iron tea table and spread the broken wax on this, and, with the help of a spirit lamp, we were able to heat the top of the table sufficiently to melt the wax to the required consistency. Longer time was given to preparing the tin foil, while with wedge-shaped slips of wood we drove the tin foil well home where the cuttings were deepest, and the wax now being softer, it could more easily be pushed well into the crevices. A plaster of Paris backing would have effectually prevented any sagging, but we had promised Professor Maspero not to allow any gypsum to be taken into the temple, lest a careless workman might spill some upon the wall itself. A second and thicker layer of wax over the first did some good ; but, as the stones on the wall are not perfectly level, there were bound to be hollows between the impression and the flat board upon which we laid it, and a sagging down to the level of the board was bound to take place as soon as the warmth of the atmosphere had again softened the beeswax. This would not have been of much consequence had we only wanted an individual stone, as there is no great gain to the appearance of the relief from its not being cut on a quite level surface, but where some two hundred stones forming this bit of wall required casting, it was of the greatest importance that the joints should be flush. A limb of a god, for instance, would look singularly out, if a half-inch projection where the stones met broke the continuity of its outline. The hollows also would not sink equally down to the level of the backing board, for one cannot ensure an even temperature of the air. The cast from the second impression was much sharper and better than the first attempt, but a movement in the wax matrix had certainly taken place, for a straight edge applied to the cast did not tally with one applied to the original stone, and it would entail some paring away of the surface to make its edges everywhere flush with those of its neighbours when they came to be embedded in the wall of the New York Museum. To amend this I resorted to the following plan :—I had my boards cut to the size of the different stones, allowing the tinfoil sheet to slightly overlap the stone to be impressed, and before the layers of wax had time to harden, from the colder surface of the stone, I had the board pressed firmly on to the back of the impression, and bent the overlapping wax over three edges of the board. When sufficiently hardened, I took the mould from the wall, and, turning it upside down, I ran melted wax into any hollows there might be between the back of the impression and the surface of the board. This effectually prevented the sagging, and did away with the necessity of tooling the surface of the casts ; for, however well the latter might be done, it was not the markings of my chisel, but those of the skilled workmen of the eighteenth dynasty which the public would desire to see.

To instruct the peasants who were my assistants in an art that I had first to learn myself was no easy matter with my very imperfect knowledge of Arabic. Currelly gave me all the assistance he could, but, after the advent of Professor Naville, the opening of the tomb at the Mentuhotep temple monopolised all his time and thoughts. However, I found the half-dozen Arabs, whose work I was directing, were quick at learning and took a great interest in their occupation. As better results were obtained we increased their pay, and by the time I was satisfied that the casts were as good as one could wish their pay had risen to treble what they received while on the dig. Be it said that the wages from "el Kompania," as they call the Egyptian Exploration Fund, are extremely low, and less than the earnings of labourers employed on any other class of work, which gave me a shrewd suspicion that the chances of concealing scarabs or other small antiquities about their person is an inducement to them to work at so low a wage.

By an increase of pay it does not follow that their hands would be kept from picking and stealing, for the "fellah," whom you might trust with anything else, is not to be trusted for an

instant with an 'antika,' which he has come to regard as his inalienable right.

The colouring of these casts, combined with their production, was very interesting; but it was absorbing an amount of my time and attention that boded ill for my water-colour work. To remedy this it was agreed that I should give up the whole day to my castings, counting two months as one, and so be able to devote all my time to my water-colour work when the "Expedition to Punt" should be completed.

The reader has now heard so much of these reproductions that a few pages about the originals and the temple they adorn may not be out of place.

Makerē-Hatshepsu is the first woman, of whom we have any historical records, who was placed in the position of ruler of a great country. Daughter of Thothmes I., her chief claim to the succession lay in her being also the daughter of Ahmes, who was descended from a long line of Theban princes. Her two half-brothers, known as Thothmes the second and third of that name, both disputed this claim. Though of less royal blood than their half-sister, their sex was better suited to their countrymen's ideas of kingship. Of the brothers, Thothmes II. had the higher claim as to birth, his mother being a princess, though not of so exalted a rank as Ahmes; while Thothmes III. was the son of an obscure concubine. The latter circumstance would have put the third claimant completely out of court but for his marriage with his half-sister. For a short while these two ruled conjointly, and while Thothmes was enlarging the temple at Karnak, Hatshepsu began the building of this sanctuary, which she dedicated to Ammon. The country suffered from the divided councils of the co-regents, an opportunity by which Thothmes II. did not fail to profit. The Queen was for a time deposed by her husband, and by his orders her image was erased from the walls of her yet unfinished temple. The party attached to the second Thothmes placed this poor creature on the throne, whereupon he further obliterated the inscriptions that referred to his half-sister. His reign was a short one, and at his death the party attached to Hatshepsu were strong enough to place her on the throne and to keep her husband in check. She ruled supreme during the rest of her life, and the beautifying of her temple was her chief concern.

The priests of Ammon, who strongly upheld her claims, now sought to strengthen her prestige in the eyes of the people. In the north colonnade the story of her divine birth is depicted: her earthly father, Thothmes I., is entirely set aside, and this beautiful series of bas-reliefs represents Ahmes in the presence of Ammon Ra, and the hieroglyphics record the words of the god, who tells her, "Hatshepsu shall be the name of this my daughter (to be born). . . . She shall exercise the kingship in this whole land." The ram-headed Khnum leads her away from the divine presence. The babe is represented further on, and the divine potter fashions its double. To lessen the prejudices against a woman sitting on the throne which had never before been occupied but by a man, the new-born child was depicted as a boy, and when, further on, the queen is crowned by the gods, she is represented with a beard and the short skirt of a king. Thothmes only appears in the final scene where he, before the assembled court, acknowledges her as the ruler of the land. The inscriptions are here framed by the queen's party for the purpose of making her position doubly sure. They represent her predecessor, whom it would now be blasphemy to call her father, as saying, "Ye shall proclaim her word; ye shall be united at her command. He who shall do her homage shall live; he who shall speak evil in blasphemy of her majesty shall die."

Though placed here so late in the day, this story doubtless gained credence with the people, who for ages had held the Pharaohs to be bodily descendants of the sun-god. Anyhow, Hatshepsu continued to reign in spite of her sex for the rest of her life.

This was a misfortune for her country, as it required the strong arm of her husband to consolidate the empire, and, as an old man, he had to subdue the tributary states that had become unruly during the Queen's milder reign.

The land of Punt was believed to be the original home of the gods; Egyptologists place it at the extreme east of Africa,—now known as Somaliland—and from time immemorial the fruit of the myrrh trees had been brought over land from thence to be offered up as incense at the shrines of the various gods. To plant the terraces of this temple of Ammon with the myrrh trees from the land which the god is stated to have called his "place of delight," was now the chief ambition of the Queen.

Five ships were equipped and sent down the Nile to a spot where a canal connected the river with the Red Sea. These are represented in what is known as the "Expedition to Punt" colonnade, and a blue border beneath is zig-zagged across to depict water, in which swim beautifully drawn Nile fish. When these same ships have reached the shores of Punt, fish peculiar to the Red Sea swim in a similar representation of water. Men, ascending the gangways, are shown carrying myrrh trees,

Walter Tyndale

swung from poles resting on their shoulders, a heavy cargo is already seen on the decks, and some apes are walking about on the top of this. The structure and rigging of these vessels are drawn with extraordinary accuracy. In both cases the ships overlap each other, the spacing of the vertical lines of the masts is well thought out to enhance the decorative quality of the reliefs, and, where these ships are under sail, the pictorial value of the curves of swelled-out canvas is well felt. An American tourist, who was inspecting these inscriptions, was very much struck by a feature in the construction of these vessels. He said he was connected with yacht building, and he noticed here a means lately adopted in America to strengthen the hull, by means of a cable stretched tight along the whole of its length. Bare spaces in the background are decorated with hieroglyphics telling the story of this expedition.

The south wall which forms the angle with the retaining wall of the terrace takes us into the land of Punt. We see here the emissaries of the queen being received by the Puntite ruler ; the stone depicting his absurdly corpulent wife is unfortunately not here, but in the Cairo Museum. Short-horned cattle, intended as gifts, now follow ; and a Punt village, with the houses raised on piles in the water, reaches to the end of this wall. In rows above, natives are carrying incense trees towards the ships, and their type, differing from the Egyptian, was no doubt carefully studied from the few Puntites who accompanied the expedition back to Thebes. Many stones in this wall are missing, and are in different collections in Europe; their interest there, as broken and disconnected fragments, is slight compared to what it would be if placed in their proper setting here. More has probably been done in one century by these collections to rob the ancient monuments of Egypt of their decorations than has been done by the Mohammedans during the twelve centuries they have been in this country.

The colour in parts has almost disappeared as portions of these walls were for a long time exposed to the weather, and though rain is of rare occurrence, during so long a lapse of time enough would have fallen to wash away some of the pigments. But where a protecting drift of sand has acted as a shelter the colour is still quite fresh. The red and yellow ochres have stood the light, but are in places worn away by the sand that has been blown against the walls. The blacks have entirely gone where they have been exposed for years to the sun, and the blues and greens have gone in most places, save in the deep cuttings.

Where these paintings have been protected from

rain, sun, and more or less from the wind, they have all the freshness of colour they had 3500 years ago, when the artists in Hatshepsu's employ were adorning her sanctuary.

There appears to have been but little mixture of pigments. A flat, conventional tint would be laid on each object represented by the relief, without attempting any realisation of the exact hue, but these colours were so disposed over the whole wall as to make a very handsome decoration. A fragment, where neither sun, rain, nor any other cause has subdued the crude pigments, is often unbeautiful in itself, but as a part of a large decorative scheme it could not be bettered; and often these causes of deterioration have so blended the colours of an individual stone that it has become an object of extreme beauty.

It would indeed be a graceful act if any owners of the missing portions of the wall representing the Land of Punt were to return these to their original setting. The writer would willingly supply them with a cast of the same, coloured so that none but an expert would know the difference, and he feels sure that Mr. Weigall would be only too happy to restore the originals to the blanks upon the wall to which they by right belong. Mr. Somers Clarke, the honorary architect to the Egyptian Exploration Fund, has reconstructed the missing portions of the colonnading that shelters these unique reliefs, and Mr. Howard Carter spent two years in carrying out this work of preservation. More remains to be done to protect the reliefs still exposed to the weather on the third terrace, but I hear that this work is to be shortly taken in hand.

CHAPTER XIV

Among the Temples

In the space covered by these two temples at Dêr el-Bahri the art and life of this interesting people can be studied as it extended over a period of 3000 years. Senmut, the architect of this temple of Hatshepsu, was not able to bring the work to completion before the Queen died, and as a partisan of his employer, he probably had to fly from the scene of his operations when Thothmes III. again took the reins of government in his hands. Restorations were carried out during the following dynasty under Ramses II., showing a distinct decline in the art. A sanctuary on the upper terrace was added during the Ptolemies, and we are able to compare this later work with that of the eighteenth dynasty. The nature of the sandstone of which it is built may, to a certain extent, account for the coarser cutting of the reliefs, but the treatment of the figures, though Greek rather than Egyptian, shows a marked falling off from the high level that art had reached in the earlier period. A distinctly Greek influence is visible in the architectural design of the sanctuary, as in all the monuments remaining of the Ptolemaic times; and this is possibly an advance. It looks as though the architects had learnt their art in Greece, and had confided the carrying out of the decoration to workmen who had lost the inspiration of their native art yet had not entered into the spirit of the Grecian.

This same sanctuary became later on the chapel of an early Christian community, and its walls and roof are still blackened with the smoke from the altar candles, or the torches that lighted the sanctuary during the celebration of the Mass. This chapel is hewn out of the cliffs, and the sandstone walls and roofing were evidently used to withstand the downward pressure of the nummulite limestone above. There are traces of the base of an altar in Hatshepsu's shrine of offerings, to the left of the sanctuary, and in every case, where the heathen gods were not hidden by church furniture, their faces have been obliterated.

Walls rebuilt by these monks leave us speculating whether they enclosed dormitories or refectory. Little regard was shown for the designs of the ancient decoration; a stone with beautifully cut head of a Thothmes would be put upside down, if it fitted into the wall better that way; and the legs of a god may only support a meat-offering on the stone above. On spaces not covered with hieroglyphics or relieved by figures, one can find sentences inscribed in the cursive or hieratic writing, or in the demotic, which is a development of the latter. An inscription in Greek characters records a prayer to Aesculapius, probably scratched here by some workman brought over from Greece during the Ptolemies, while a further interest is given to this stone by an amendment of a Coptic monk, centuries later, who, after cutting a cross above this prayer, has written underneath—"No one heals but God himself." Some other Greek has cut his high-sounding name on a stone, beneath which we find "Crocodilos" written in another hand whose owner was apparently moved by the same spirit that we occasionally see evinced when the name of a Briton, scratched on a wall, is followed by—"is an ass," written by another in a lighter mood. Nineteenth century names are happily rarer here than on many monuments; for fallen masses of débris, until the century's close, had preserved these remains from modern desecration.

The view from this upper terrace is remarkably fine. Standing with your back to the overhanging cliffs, you look across a mile of the wilderness which forms a part of the Theban necropolis. The fertile plain, transversely cut by the Nile, is backed in the distance by the hills of the Arabian desert.

To the right lie the Ramesseum, with Seti's temple to the left, while, across the river, and near its banks, stand the great colonnades of Luxor and the huge pylon of Karnak.

In 1894-95 the entire temple was exhumed by Professor Naville, who gave his services, the Egyptian Exploration Fund defraying the cost of the work.

Most of my assistants in the casting of Punt increased in knowledge, and those who proved too stupid to learn returned to the "dust," as they termed the excavations. One of the remaining men showed an especial aptitude, which bespoke long practice in the manufacture of fakes—impostures—now treasured by many a tourist as gems picked up by good luck from an Arab who had got them, "*we won't say how!*" (a wink here from the tourist). This man spoke a few words of English, which I allowed him to air. I have forgotten his name, but his solemnly calling out—"Tyndale, Koom!" whenever he wished me to come and see his work, obtained him the name of "Tyndale Koom"; and as such I can only remember him. Be it explained that it was not in undue familiarity that I was so addressed; for, except when such titles as Bey or Pasha had been acquired, this rather servile creature would have addressed any of his co-religionists, whatever their position might be, by the name their parents had given them.

My next most important helper was an ex-donkey boy, who had forsaken that calling on the demise of his beast. After him in order of intelligence, I had an ex-convict ; a taciturn individual,—which quality was a comfort,—and a steady worker. I was informed that he had killed someone in a fit of rage, but that, if one knew him, he was not a bad man. It behoved me therefore not to excite his rage, and, as he did not chatter like the others, he never excited mine. One or two boys were there, either to prepare the wax or to run errands, but the necessity for these was a nuisance, for I was in constant fear lest they might damage the walls.

A very important assistant was one whom we kept down at the hut, who took the casts from the impressions. These were hard to get right, for we none of us had had much experience in handling plaster of Paris. The colouring of the casts took less time than preparing them, so I was able to devote some of my leisure to my water-colour work. The little Ptolemaic temple at Dêr el-Medîneh, hidden in some folds of the desert hills a mile south of our valley, was a subject I especially loved to paint. The Arabic "Dêr" signifies a convent, and this temple bears traces of the Coptic monks who once dwelt here. It was built in honour of Hathor, the goddess of the dead, and was also dedicated to the goddess Maat. Although the inscriptions are far inferior to those at Dêr el-Bahri, the interior lends itself to pictorial treatment perhaps better than any part of its far-famed neighbour. The calyx-headed columns and the Hathor capitals of the piers, with the doorway of the sanctuary, compose beautifully in certain lights. Traces of colour are left upon these capitals and on the winged sun-disc over the door.

Ptolemaic temples have one great advantage over the earlier ones, and that is, that they are in a much better state of preservation ; in fact, some can hardly be called ruins. Save the furniture, which is now mostly in museums, the temples of Dendera, Esneh, and Edfu stand to-day very much as they were when first erected. For grandeur they may bear the relation to the earlier work that a live mouse does to a dead lion ; but it is something to be alive !

There is much to paint at Medînet Habu, a mile further south. The twentieth dynasty decorations in the great temple of Ramses III. look extremely coarse after the delicate reliefs at Dêr el-Bahri ; but so many of the eighteenth dynasty inscriptions had been scraped off by rival factions or succeeding Pharaohs, that Ramses III. was determined that his should survive. I was at some pains to take measurements of the earlier reliefs, and I could hardly realise how shallow these were.

In the Punt series, where the background is cut away, the modelling and relief of the figures are given in a depth that never exceeds $\frac{1}{16}$th of an inch. The smaller figures are not relieved by more than $\frac{1}{32}$nd of an inch, and sometimes less. The larger figures on some of the columns are not relieved from the background, but their outlines are incised. Bold as these outlines look, I found that they never exceeded $\frac{3}{16}$th of an inch in depth, and the beautiful modelling of these figures is all within that depth, as I proved by using a straight edge across the face of the column. The reliefs of Seti I. are slightly higher at his temple at Abydos, and I can recall no work in relief of the time of Ramses II., but only incised inscriptions, which seemed to deepen during his long reign. By the time of Ramses III. I found these incisions had reached a depth of from four to five inches. The restorations of Ramses II. at Dêr el-Bahri are in relief, but it was more in imitation of that of his predecessor than quite typical of his own time. The coarser surface of the stone and the larger scale of the building might account to some extent for the inscriptions being cut deeper; but the fear of erasure must have chiefly led to this. A palimpsest—that is, an inscription cut over another —would be very difficult where the outline of a hieroglyph is nearly five inches deep and two inches wide at the surface. In the eighteenth dynasty bold relief or deep incision was understood, but was only used where an effect to be seen from a distance was sought. The bas-relief seems to have disappeared for a while after the reign of Seti I. I found it again at Karnak in a modest little temple of the twenty-fifth dynasty, and, though cut on sandstone, the modelling was extremely beautiful, for a revival in art had then set in, which, however, declined during the Persian domination. Coarse as the decoration may be in the actual cutting, the design is often very grand; there is a swing-and-go about the great battle scenes which cover some walls that is amazing. Art seemed to be making a heroic struggle for life before her decline in the next reign. Space does not allow me to enter more fully into these stirring representations, but in his *History of Egypt* Professor Breasted graphically places before his readers these records of an eventful reign which Ramses III. had inscribed on his great temple.

Passing out through the massive pylon we find on our left a series of small temples that carries us from the reign of Hatshepsu right up to one of the later Ptolemies; a period of fourteen centuries. Not a great lapse of time in the history of Egypt, but one that would in ours take us back to the Heptarchy. The walls of Hatshepsu's temple

Walter Tyndale

bear witness to her feuds with father, husband, and brother, and over her effaced pictures are inscribed the figures, or cartouches, of the three Thothmes. Possibly these served as a lesson to Ramses III. when he had the walls of his temple inscribed so deeply. We pass on through a pylon erected by Taharqa of the twenty-fifth dynasty—the Tirharkah of the Bible—and we enter a delightful little chapel of Nektanebos, the last Pharaoh of the last dynasty (thirtieth). Eight clustered papyrus columns with budded capitals once supported the roof; two only now stand in their entirety. These columns, connected by a stone screen and backed by the Taharqa pylon, make a charming group from outside, while the great pylon of the tenth Ptolemy leads us into a colonnaded vestibule, and a large courtyard ends this series of temples.

That this work of both Nektanebos and the Ptolemy were done after some of Ramses' great structure had fallen in partial ruin, is evidenced by its being carried right across the inner and outer enclosing walls of the temple area; it also encroaches on a part of the site of Ramses' pavilion. This pavilion, of which the central part only remains, forms the great entrance to the temple area. It is not a structure of great beauty, but it is very interesting, as being the only standing remains of a secular building of any importance.

As the later temples arose, so the earlier ones declined, if they were not actually in use. A quarry so near at hand, with ready cut stones, was too tempting not to be made use of; and inscriptions of the earlier temples can be traced on blocks of stone used in the later ones. It is strange that the ruins of the Christian village, east of the great temple, should show only crumbling walls of mud brick. The village church stood in the centre of the second court, and this also was built of this poor material, when so much dressed stone lay all around.

The magnificent Amenhotep III. built his sumptuous palace near these temples of Medînet Habu, but hardly a trace of this now remains; it had probably fallen into ruin when Ramses III. was erecting his great temple. That "this world is no abiding city" was more than a mere phrase in Pharaonic times is here exemplified, for amongst the numerous dwelling places prepared for the dead, or dedicated to the gods, nothing now remains standing of what was inhabited by the living. The great palaces that must have existed in Thebes, both to house the kings and the great nobles, were all built of mud-bricks, durable enough for a lifetime, but leaving nothing but some fragments of pavement by which posterity can judge of their splendours. Fortunately, we find some records of these habitations on the walls of the tombs and the temples; and specimens of the furniture, housed in the lasting abodes of the dead, give us some idea of the daily life of these people.

The pavilion of Ramses III., part of which we have now seen, suggests a fortress more than a palace, and that warrior king possibly built it in stone for strategic reasons rather than as a temporary residence.

CHAPTER XV

The Tomb of Queen Tyi

Christmas had passed, but the sing-song and dust behind the Mentuhotep temple showed that the work there was still in full swing. The great shaft was not yet cleared, and with every ton of débris that was thrown out we heard some fresh theory. My own humble suggestion that it was probably a sewer, and that the find might prove to be a dynastic cesspool, was received with all the contempt that it deserved. The interest in what might happen at the dig in the next valley had gone down to zero. " Oh, just turning over rubbish that has been sifted over and over again ! " " It will keep them amused, and Weigall will see that they do no mischief," were the expressions of thoughts more consoling to the thinker than satisfying to my curiosity. This valley of the tombs of the kings ; the mystery of which thousands of tourists, picnickers, and the electric light had not been able to destroy ; a spot that I

Walter Tyndale

was daily longing to revisit, would but this work on Punt allow me the leisure, must surely yet contain many secrets that pick and shovel, ably directed, might at any time divulge. News travels with amazing speed in the East, and tidings of a find there would not take long to cross the mountain that separates Dêr el-Bahri from the Biban el-Mulûk. Ayrton, let him do his work ever so quietly, could not stop a thousand native tongues from wagging; and wag they did, to great purpose, one fine morning. The very air seemed thick with news! News that Ayrton was knee-deep in gold and precious stones, feverishly filling empty petroleum tins, pickle pots and cans from Chicago, with the spoil, was the very least that one's imagination could conjure up. The work on Punt went leisurely that day, for "Tyndale Koom," Ahmet, and even the silent ex-convict, were chattering all the time. "Oh, shut up, and get on with your work!" from me would quiet them for a bit, and whisperings would be exchanged instead of loud arguments. Needless to say the archæological value of the find did not interest them in the least. That every one connected with these excavations is doing it simply for the plunder, is a rooted idea in the native mind which neither proof nor argument can disturb. That the share of spoil which "Mistrr Davis" or "Mistrr Eirton" would get would allow them to retire, sip coffee and play backgammon for the rest of their lives, was what exercised their minds, and possibly roused a good deal of secret resentment—that these dogs of Christians should be permitted to carry off what Allah had clearly intended should fall to the lot of the true believer ! These sentiments would only be expressed when I was out of hearing, for I had had some influence in getting the Mudir to increase their wages, and had put in a word for them when baksheesh was to be distributed.

One thing, however, was certain, the tomb of Queen Tyi had been found and opened. The massive limestone cliffs that form the barrier between the two digs might have been but a gauze curtain, so marvellously we heard of our neighbours' doings. Mr. Theodore Davis had ridden over from his dahabiyeh ; the Bash Moufetish, with his 'wakeel' and extra guards, had arrived ; telegrams had been dispatched to M. Maspero ; a special artist was on the spot, and a photographer had been summoned from Cairo. The arrival of our friend Ayrton, when the day's work was over, cleared the air. His face bore the expression of a gentle angler who, having landed a big fish, joins his companions who have done no more than lose their tackle. He might well feel pleased, for, when we learnt the full truth, it was evident that his find was one of the most dramatic for a good many years. He told us that the tomb had certainly been opened since first Queen Tyi had been laid to rest there; but there was evidence that this had not been done for plunder, as no valuables had been abstracted, but some hieroglyphs referring to the heresy which she had fostered and her son had tried to establish, had been effaced. It seemed evident that this had been done but a few years after the Queen's death, and that after the priests of Ammon had satisfied their religious zeal, and had repaired the breach they had made in the wall, Tyi had slept undisturbed for over three thousand years. A landslip from the mountain in whose bosom she lay had protected her from the plunder of the Roman, the fanaticism of the early Christians, and the greed of the Arabs, but had now failed to conceal her resting-place from the Egyptologist.

The talk of Queen Tyi, of her son Akhnaton, and the religious revolution of their times, was the absorbing topic of that evening. It was disappointing to hear that we should not be allowed to see the tomb for some days, as the photographer was away from Cairo, and nothing could be touched until careful photographs had been taken of everything in the position in which it had been found. The fear, also, of what might happen during that time was considerable; for though objects may remain intact for centuries in the equable temperature of a rock tomb ; they may crumble into dust when touched, or even when merely exposed to the more variable outside atmosphere. These fears were to a certain extent justified, as we shall see later on.

A week elapsed before any one, except those immediately concerned, was allowed to visit the tomb. An American artist, J. Lindon Smith, who was commissioned to paint the interior with its valuable contents, would drop in at our camp on his way back to Luxor, and excite our curiosity to a yet higher pitch by telling us of his day's work. Long hours spent in this death-chamber had not damped his spirits, for he was one of the most amusing companions it has been my good fortune to meet. Four fine canopic jars had been found, portraits of the Queen forming their stoppers ; also a box of beautiful blue glazed toilet ornaments.

Before we visit the mortal remains of this romantic queen, it will be of interest to some who are not well versed in Egyptian history, to get some idea of the important *rôle* she played during the eighteenth Dynasty, when the Empire had reached the zenith of its power. Unlike her predecessor, Hatshepsu, she was of unknown birth, and it is stated that she was not an Egyptian, but there seems little authority for this. She married the young Pharaoh, Amenhotep III., about the time of

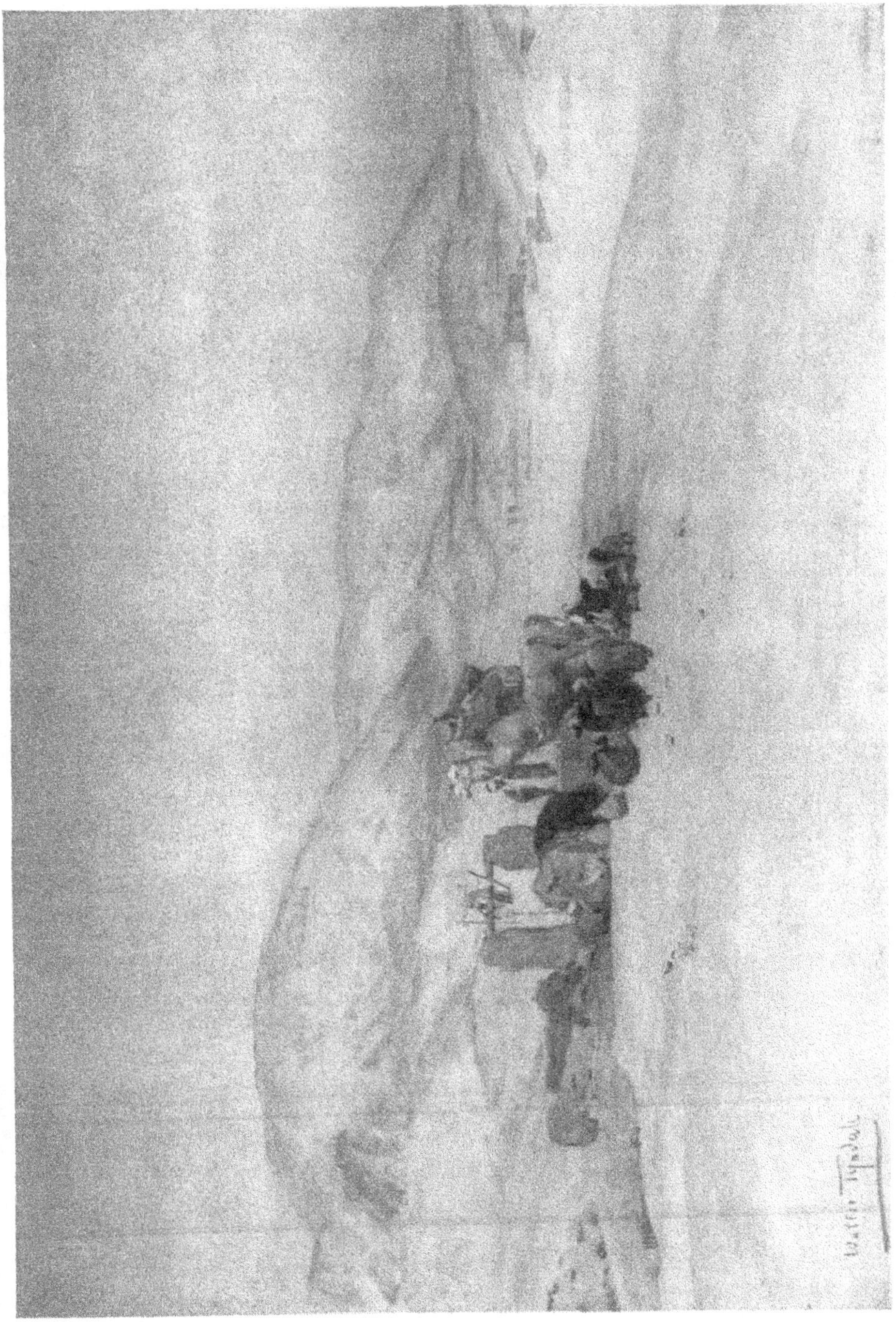
Walter Tyndale

his accession, and this magnificent prince leaves many records which declare her to be the "Queen Consort"; and the royal titulary closes with these words: "She is the wife of a Mighty King, whose southern boundary is as far as Karoy and northern as far as Naharin." As Breasted remarks in his *History of Egypt*: "it was as if to remind any who might reflect on the humble origin of the Queen of the exalted station she now occupied." Thothmes III. and his two warrior successors had consolidated the Empire over which Amenhotep was born to rule; highly cultured, and with a full treasury at his command, this Amenhotep made Thebes the greatest capital the world has ever seen. Nothing now remains of his great palace save some fragments scattered about in the different museums; a few stones mark the site of his mortuary temple; and the Colossi have been so ill-used by time that one is impressed by little more than their stupendous size.

Of still standing monuments, the large temple of Luxor gives one the best idea of what great things were done during this reign. The architect, Amenhotep, son of Hapi, was known to the Greeks twelve centuries later; and the wisdom of his sayings are quoted in *The Proverbs of the Seven Wise Men.* His striking portrait may be seen in the Cairo Museum.

Contrary to the customs of the country, the

queen took a prominent part both in state and religious ceremonials, and it is curious to think of this delicately-made, dainty little woman, suggesting a creation of Botticelli, watching these religious rites whilst she secretly fostered a heresy that was to cause the downfall of this great Empire during the reign of her son. The causes that led to this reformation are not recorded, the priests of Ammon, who were all-powerful, were not likely to advertise the discontent that may have been felt, and if the Augurs laughed, they laughed in secret. Her influence may have been felt by her husband, but it was everything to her son; and it was left to this youth, when he succeeded his father, to wage war against the power of the priesthood and boldly to declare the existence of one Supreme Being, whose physical manifestation was the sun-disc. His very name, Amenhotep IV., became impossible to him;—"Ammon rests"—how could he be called this when he was effacing the name of Ammon from the walls of every temple and was building a shrine to the new god Aton? "Akh en-Aton," meaning "Spirit of Aton," should be his name from henceforth. For six years he struggled to stamp out the worship of Ammon, but the links with the past were too strong in Thebes to be easily broken. With his mother and the priest, Eye, who had ever encour aged his reforming zeal, he set out to build a new capital, which he would dedicate to Aton. He chose a site some three hundred miles below Thebes, now known as Tell el-Amarna, but which he called "Akhetaten," "Horizon of Aton." Here it appears he lived for the rest of his life, like the Pope in the Vatican, not willing to set foot on any land that was not specially dedicated to his god. Tribute soon ceased to come in from his Asiatic provinces, and at the close of his reign the Empire had dwindled down to that portion which is watered by the Nile. He left no sons, and was succeeded by his son-in-law, Sakere, of whom little is known. Another son-in-law, Twet-ankh-Amon, succeeded the former one, and after a while compromised with the priests of Ammon and returned to Thebes, which for twenty years had seen no Pharaoh. It was probably during this reign, when the cult of Ammon was restored, that Queen Tyi's tomb was entered and every reference to the accursed Aton was obliterated.

The time at last arrived when we were allowed to see this queen before her bejewelled mummy-case should be sent to Cairo and her bones once more walled up in her niche at the foot of the overhanging cliff. My friends, Mr. Henry Holiday, Miss Mothersole, and I were the favoured ones that morning. We were not long in climbing the mountain and descending into the valley of the Tombs of the Kings. A couple of trousered policemen keeping guard indicated the spot we were seeking; and when satisfied that we were friends of the "Hawaga" we were conducted down a slope that led to the newly-opened chamber. On peeping in my first impressions were those of surprise at the incongruity of the scene that I then beheld. An athletic and beflannelled young Englishman, with the aid of an electric burner and surrounded by tin cigarette boxes, was sorting precious stones; the light which caused the glitter on these fell also on a part of the whited walls of this sepulchre, and the grim shadow that our friend cast might have been that of a ghoul or a priest of Ammon. Gold and white were the prevailing colours of all that caught the electric rays, and at the first glance it looked more like a wrecked boudoir of Napoleonic times than a mysterious abode of the dead.

These reflections were of short duration, for the handful of stones were soon stowed away: half moon-shaped bits of lapis-lazuli in a box of "Egyptian Beauties," cornelian and turquoise respectively in tins from Demetrius or Nestor Genakalis; and Ayrton hastened to welcome us and to assist us into the tomb, which was several

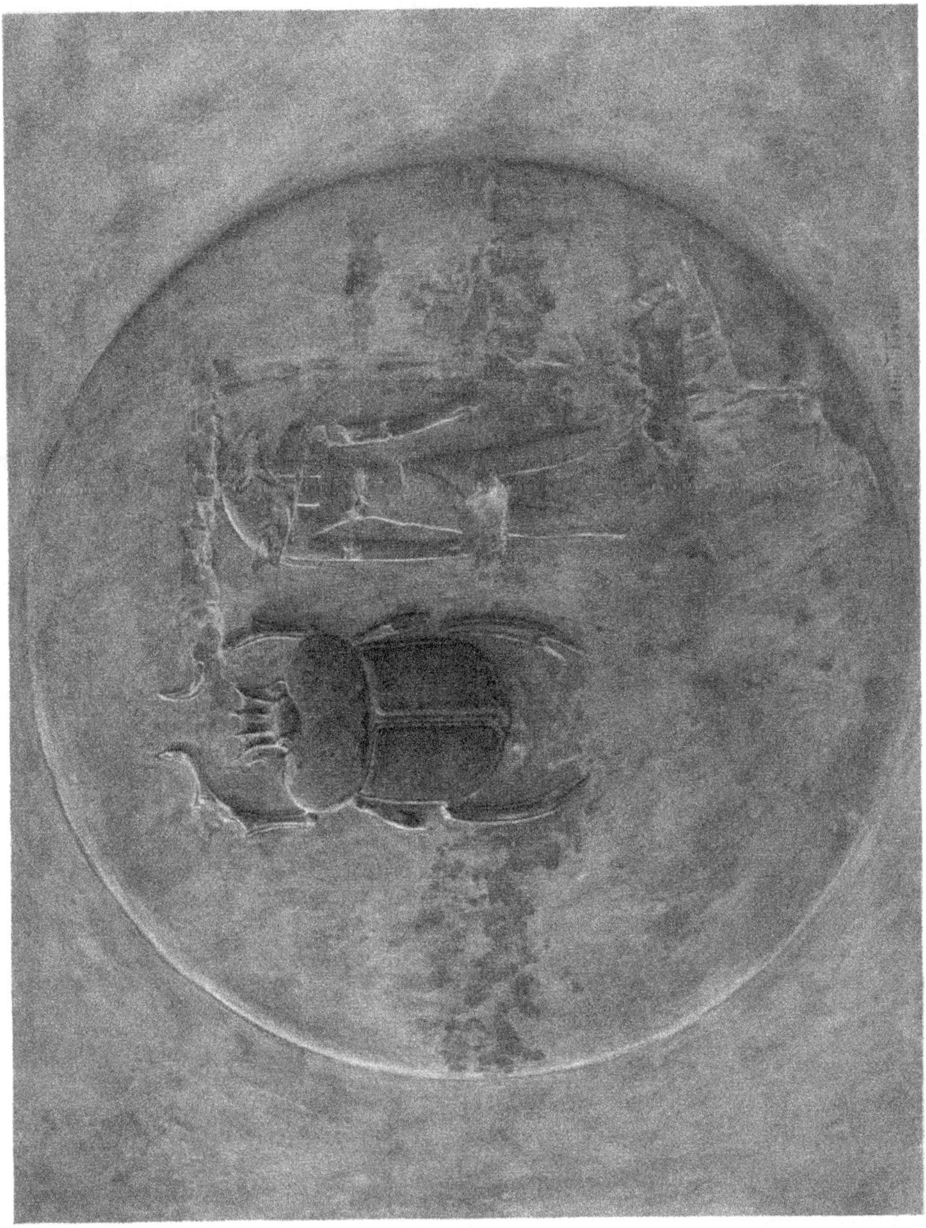

feet lower than the opening into it. We had to move with great caution, and to be careful to touch nothing, as most of the furniture was so brittle that a false step might have caused incalculable damage. The fallen canopy had so far blocked our view of the mummy-case. A safe place being found where we could stand without injuring anything, the light was shifted, and there before us lay the effigy of Tyi. It was the most thrilling sight I ever beheld. Arrayed as she might have been when Amenhotep the Magnificent led her to the marriage feast, there she lay, with arms folded, and that immovable expression on her face which the contemplation of the vanity of all things might have produced. Dazzled by the splendour of this sight I did not at first notice that the side of the coffin had fallen out, and that alongside this gorgeous effigy lay the real body of the queen. Her dried-up face, sunken cheeks, and thin, leathery-looking lips, exposing a few teeth, were in ghastly contrast to the golden diadem which encircled her head and the gold necklace that partially hid her shrunken throat. Her body was wrapped in thin gold plate, but this being broken and torn made it yet more horrible to look at. An uncomfortable feeling that it was unchivalrous to stare at the poor creature when she was looking so far from her best brought me back to her effigy on the mummy-case with a mental apology that I regretted having taken her unawares, and would in future only think of her as she appeared in all her glory.

Now, the reason why the body lay outside the coffin requires a word of explanation. This heavy case had rested on a beautiful trestle, surmounted by a gilded canopy, but, at some unknown period, one of the carved legs of this trestle had given way, the coffin had fallen on the floor with sufficient force to burst the side of it, and the mummy had rolled out. *Sic transit gloria mundi !*

Before this book is in print nearly all the contents of Tyi's tomb will have been ticketed and catalogued for the inspection of the next season's crop of tourists when their dragoman shows them round the Cairo Museum. The queen herself will, I am glad to say, not be there. While everything that had any archæological or artistic value was being carried down to Mr. Davis' dahabiyeh, I learnt that the body itself was not to be removed, and that the tomb would be again walled up. Though shorn of every emblem of royalty, may she sleep as peacefully for the next three thousand years as she has slept since the priests of Ammon disturbed her sacred rest !

I wrote the above account while the excitement

of this dramatic find was filling our minds, and while our enthusiasm was untroubled by any doubts as to its authenticity. I will let it stand ; for first impressions have a freshness which no subsequent remembered sensations can hope to possess.

But a sad disillusionment was in store. Since I left Egypt this interesting mummy has been examined by expert surgeons in addition to the Egyptologists, and the skeleton has proved to be that of a young man of from twenty-five to twenty-six years of age.

There can be no doubt that the furniture of the sepulchre is that of the tomb of Queen Tyi, but where her bones now rest and who this young man is who has usurped her place are problems which remain unsolved. It seems scarcely possible that these are the mortal remains of Ikhnaton brought here from Tel-el-Amarna to lie near his forefathers. His eventful reign could hardly have ended when he was but twenty-five years old. Will further evidence come to light of the doings of the priests of Ammon when they opened the sepulchre and erased the hated name of Aton ? Or was this a mock burial of the queen whose body may have been taken to her son's city of Akhetaton to be safe from the desecrating hands of the priests ?

We must leave these questions unanswered and return to the dig at the Mentuhotep temple.

CHAPTER XVI

The Mentuhotep Temple

Towards the close of the first month of 1907 the bottom of the shaft was reached, and, 600 feet from the entrance, it led into the mortuary chamber. Recessed into the left wall stood the resting-place of the mummy. This formed a small inner chamber high enough to stand in and deep enough to hold a sarcophagus. It was gable-roofed, with the open gable end facing the room we first entered. Large slabs of alabaster lined the walls, and though no inscriptions were here to throw any light upon the subject, it was evidently the sepulchre of an exalted personage. The hopeless confusion of the contents showed that it had been plundered; nothing that thieves could easily convert into money was left, and the floor was littered with broken bits of mummy-case, pieces of bows and arrows, wooden figures, and a number of earthenware pots. In one corner a brown heap

of dust with shreds of mummy-cloth was all that was visible of the body which this tomb was so carefully built to conceal. The heat was so great that the wax candles we held bent and softened in our hands. We had left most of our clothes outside, and though we had little enough on, that little was almost unbearable. The enclosed air was stifling, and the desire to get out dominated all other sensations. The dramatic sight which we had witnessed in the tomb in the neighbouring valley was absent here ; the heap of brown dust lying in the corner awakened no more feelings of awe than a sackful of guano shot there might have done, and what little vitality remained to us after breathing this fœtid atmosphere was required to crawl up the long shaft to get into the open air. That brown heap was probably the remains of Mentuhotep, but one must be cautious in making such assertions.

It was, anyhow, an important find ; and as, day by day, the contents of the mortuary chamber were brought up to the hut, it became increasingly evident that they had been intended for the furniture of a royal tomb. The sorting and packing of all these things took some time, and our nightly attempts to piece the broken fragments together had to be abandoned, as there seemed no end to their number.

Another tomb to the left of the great shaft was found, as more débris was cleared at the foot of the cliffs, and the huge granite sarcophagus it contained, and its situation near the sanctuary of the temple, suggests its having once contained a royal mummy.

Mrs. Naville was for weeks occupied in arranging and sorting the fragments belonging to seven little shrines that had stood on the upper terrace, and enough remained to enable her son-in-law to reconstruct on paper a completed one. The design was very beautiful, and the sculptured ornamentation on some of the fragments nearly equalled the work of the XVIII dynasty. The drawing of the figures on parts of the remaining walls of the terraces is inferior to the later work, being more the conventional tradition of skilled workmen than the living art of personal genius, such as one sees in the Hatshepsu temple. It is to be regretted that one of these beautiful little shrines could not have been reconstructed and allowed to remain *in situ* as a fine example of XI dynasty work. As fragments they will now help to fill some shelves in different museums, but their value as a piece of architectural design will be very small. To have left one would, however, have entailed the erection of an iron framework to protect it from the natives, and standing as it would have done in an iron cage, its effect among these ruins would have been rather incongruous. Were it possible to make the receiving of stolen fragments an indictable offence, or to enforce such laws as exist, these interesting records might often be allowed to remain in their proper surroundings: but it is a difficult matter ensuring the safety of these works of art in a country where public opinion is not alive to their true value. If a thief is caught in possession of stolen antiquities, it is almost impossible to get a conviction from a native magistrate, who is ready to do a deal in antiquities himself. As an instance of how venial a sin the stealing of an 'antika' is considered by others than natives, the following may illustrate. A lady, who before being attacked by the collector's mania would not have stolen a pin, brought a scarab to our camp, and asked Currelly to help her to decipher the cartouche and also to appraise its value. Currelly decided that it was a sham, very much to the lady's disappointment; but, loath to believe that she had been taken in, she gave her reasons for still maintaining its genuineness: "Achmet" (the donkey boy) "assured me that he had stolen it from the dig, and he has such an honest face that I am sure he was speaking the truth!" When the laughter had subsided—even that of her husband—it dawned on the good lady that there was something a bit out in her argument, and that possibly dear Achmet was not a thief in spite of his honest face.

There is something about 'antika' collecting that distorts the moral vision. A man will sip coffee with an 'antika' dealer while he is buying goods that he knows have been stolen from him, whereas he would have the man locked up were he a receiver of a stolen pair of boots. When Currelly first joined the excavations at Thebes and was less able than now to detect a "Kurnah-made" scarab, he wished to have his own judgment corroborated while making some purchases at a dealer's in Luxor. The foreman, or 'reis,' as they are called, of the excavations was a Kurnah man, and doubtlessly a deft hand at forging 'antikas' himself, so it struck Currelly that it might be advisable to take this man with him to the shop and get him to drop a hint should he detect any "Kurnah-made" fakes. The foreman fell in with this, and as Currelly treated his men kindly, and had had some experience in handling natives, he felt that he could depend on his ally. A tempting lot of 'antikas' were spread out on the counter, and our friend began making his selection. "Now, how about this?" he would ask, picking up a blue-glazed 'ushabti,' "Can you guarantee its genuineness?" The salesman assured him, by the beard of the Prophet, that he knew the very tomb where it had been found, and appealed to his co-religionist, the foreman, for corroboration. The latter, wishing to serve his master, and yet not to make an enemy of the shopman, would also swear by all he held holy that such a bit of blue glaze was beyond the skill of the forger, and that he could vouch for the tomb where it had been found; but a gentle stamp on Currelly's foot under the counter was a sufficient reminder that the foreman was only lying *par complaisance*, and the purchase of the 'ushabti' was not made.

Should the next article be a genuine one, the protestations of the dealer would again be corroborated by the 'reis,' and an accompanying elbow movement of the latter was a hint to Currelly that he might safely buy. This would then be set aside as worth bargaining for. So it went on, until every 'antika' that was worth a place in the museum in which Currelly was interested had been sifted out. As the protestations of the 'reis' and the dealer grew more eloquent over a sham that was offered for sale, so the foot-stamping increased in vigour, and Currelly was thankful that his foot was protected by a substantial boot. The long process of bargaining would then begin for each individual object; then an offer for the lot if taken *en bloc*. "Can you expect me to sell for so much less than I gave?" would say the dealer as one appealing to the better side of a stern client. "But, as it is for you—and mind you, no one else," with a shake of the finger, I am prepared to only lose so much." This kindness would end that day's proceedings. Subtle signs had doubtlessly been exchanged between the dealer and his co-religionist as to the latter's commission when in course of time the deal would be concluded; for however loyal the service of the 'reis' had been, baksheesh is baksheesh, and baksheesh is as essential a part of trading in the East as advertising is in the West. It would not be safe to allow the bargaining to stretch over more than a week or two, as it would be bringing it dangerously near the tourist season, and a more advantageous offer from one of the "Sawarhine" would mean the loss of the lot; but when the season is well over a bargain can be allowed with safety to stretch over a month or two.

It is, however, only fair to say that there are dealers who trade in a more straightforward manner, and who, having a reputation to lose, will not risk it by palming off a fraud, knowing it to be such.

Towards the end of March the reflected rays from the cliffs made the valley of Dêr el-Bahri uncomfortably hot. When we had a spell of south wind the heat rose to such an extent that the impressions could only be taken from daybreak to

Walter Tyndale

ten o'clock at the latest, as the wax would not harden later in the day. The casting was often deferred till sundown, and carried on well into the night. I was anxious that the casting of "Punt" should be completed this season, though I was obliged to defer a great part of the colouring till the next; therefore, when the wind shifted to a cooler quarter, the work would go on all day.

The men were pleased enough to be able to sleep in the shade during the heat of the day when the "khamsîn" was on. The tombs were the only cool places I could find to do some water-colour work in. My subjects were sometimes almost invisible after first coming from the glare outside, but they would appear light enough to work at when my eyes got accustomed to the diminished light. It was, of course, only in such parts of the tombs as were near the entrance where this was possible, unless one used artificial lighting.

The illustration is from a wall painting in the tomb of Nakht, one of those sepulchres to which I briefly alluded, that the visitor to Dêr el-Bahri passes after leaving the Ramesseum; should he refer to his Baedeker, he will see it marked No. 125 on the plan given of the tombs of Sheik Abd el-Kurnah, and the guide-book also gives a full description of the scenes depicted on the walls of this and the other tombs which form the interesting group in the

Theban necropolis. Not much is known of Nakht himself beyond what these walls tell us. He is alluded to as a scribe, and was probably a priest of Ammon, or connected with that powerful body of men, which was so important a factor in the destinies of the New Empire. He lived about the time of Hatshepsu, and during his lifetime the preparation of his final earthly resting place had evidently interested him keenly. He had seen enough of animal or bird-headed gods and goddesses, and probably valued them at their true worth, and he preferred that his spirit should live amongst the scenes where his heart was fixed. References to Ammon were there, for a belief in a bodily manifestation of the Supreme Being was probably always held, even when the Augurs were laughing. By a curious irony of fate, these references were later on ruthlessly defaced by the Pharaoh whose one great object in life was to substitute for the worship of the host of Theban gods that of a god made manifest in the sun-disk. The letter offended Ikhnaton more than the spirit, for he could not dissociate the name of Ammon from the priesthood which he was trying to crush.

Nakht's pleasures were those of most well-to-do country gentlemen. He is depicted supervising farming operations, from the ploughing and sowing of the land to the winnowing of the ripened corn.

He is also shown personally seeing to the vintage and the wine-pressing. Judging from the excellence of the representations, sport must have been his chief delight, the panel, where he is spearing fish, and where birds are being caught among the marsh growth, is most decorative. You may also see him and his wife at table, while his cat is eating a fish which was probably not prepared to Nakht's liking, and, surrounded by his household, he is entertained by dancers and musicians.

I chose three of the latter representations as an illustration, partly because they were in a good state of preservation, and also because the wall they are on received enough daylight for my purpose. The costumes of these ladies were well suited to the high temperature!

The limestone of the rocks in which these tombs are cut is a coarser quality than that at Dêr el-Bahri, and had been prepared with a cement before the colour was put on. The delicate cutting of the low reliefs in the Hatshepsu temple had to be abandoned, and a slight attempt at shading was resorted to here to relieve the figures. The effect is not so good, and defective parts where bits of the cement have been knocked off, or are detaching themselves from the wall, give it a look of shabbiness that is never noticeable in the reliefs cut in the stone itself, be they ever so much damaged by time or wilful mischief. They show, however, the skilled draughtsmanship of the designer more than where the sculptor has cut away the outline. These figures, some fifteen inches high, are drawn with a very free hand; the contour of a limb is often done with but two pulls of the brush. The strings of the harp look simple enough, but my efforts to pull each one off with one stroke, as in the original, made me appreciate the dexterity of Nakht's artist. Indeed, he may have been his own artist, for the term "scribe" probably included both painter and sculptor. This idea gained on me while working in the tomb. The artists who drew the beautiful eighteenth or nineteenth dynasty figures must have disliked substituting a jackal's head for that of a man's, as in Anubis, or surmounting a lovely figure of Hathor with the face of a cow. In decorating his own tomb he could do as he liked; and no monstrous faces disfigure this last resting-place of Nakht. Passages from *The Book of that which is in the Underworld* or from *The Book of the Portals* are absent here; he had had to treat of them *ad nauseam* while serving in the temples. His soul should wander about his fields and vineyards, and be refreshed with the good things of his table while long-eyed damsels discoursed sweet music.

There are many tombs of greater importance

than this of Nakht; to attempt to describe these is not within the scope of this book. All should visit that of Rekhmerē, where the pictures speak for themselves.

The casting of "Punt" was drawing to a close, and a continuance of hot wind decided me to get out of this burning valley of Dêr el-Bahri. I had not seen Abydos when an opportunity of staying close to Seti's temple presented itself. Mr. Garstang, who was directing some excavations in the cemetery close by, kindly invited me to join his camp. The temple is eight and a half miles from the river, just beyond the reach of the cultivated land, and the nearest station is that of Beliâneh. Though the camp is only some eighty miles from the one at Dêr el-Bahri, it entailed a long journey and a night spent at Luxor to enable me to catch a stopping train leaving soon after daybreak. The wind happily had shifted to a cooler quarter or I should have been half-stifled in the train. We crawled along the east bank of the Nile for about half of the way, and crossed over to the west side at Nag Hamâdeh. Long stoppages at stations where no one got in and no passengers alighted enabled the company to make this run of eighty miles spread over five or six hours. I secured a couple of donkeys at Beliâneh to take me and my luggage across the cultivation. The sun was now so high in the heavens that the whole of one's person fell within the shadow of the brim of one's helmet. But a week had elapsed since the corn first began to lose its spring greenness, and now it looked ready for the reaping hook. The colour of the landscape was therefore much finer, and the expanse of golden crops to right and left made the desert hills look silvery by contrast.

The temple of Seti is reached soon after leaving the plain. Its interior is disappointing and does not lend itself to a sketch. A quarter of a mile further in the desert is the ruined temple of Ramses II. Save these two temples and the cemetery beyond, nothing visible remains of the ancient city of Abydos. Most of it must have disappeared when Strabo visited Egypt, for he speaks of it as "once a great city, second only to Thebes, but now only a small place."

After crossing some low hills strewn with broken pottery, and here and there an open pit tomb nearly silted up with sand, we dipped down into a sandy plain shut in by the Libyan hills to the west. A Union Jack hanging limp over a one-storied mud-brick house marked my destination.

The excavating which Garstang is carrying out at the cost of the Liverpool University, is likely to last several years, which made it worth while to build comfortable quarters for the members of the

dig, and a substantial storehouse for the finds. My host had run down to Cairo for a few days, but Mr. Harold Jones and Mr. Blackman were superintending the work. Howard Carter also was staying there, bent on the same work as I had come to do—to make some studies of the Seti bas-reliefs. The house was planned with great skill, to keep the living room cool and to accommodate six people, without unduly drawing on the funds at the disposal of the excavation, and the lunch showed that Harold Jones could keep house as well as plan one. Having had nothing since a hurried breakfast at five a.m., I was able to do this meal full justice. The heat is so great that as the season advances the afternoon "siesta" grows from a luxury into a necessity. Work becomes impossible from one till four; it is therefore well to shorten one's rest at night and resume it in the early afternoon.

CHAPTER XVII

KARNAK

I HAD the advantage of Howard Carter's company on my first visit to the Seti temple. His long experience in drawing the temple inscriptions has given him a better knowledge of Egyptian art than possibly any of our contemporaries.

Though art had reached its highest point during the eighteenth dynasty, the reliefs in this temple show no signs of its decadence, and I am inclined to place them as the greatest achievements in pictorial art that Egypt has left us. They are the work of a great artist who, though still imbued with the traditions of the previous dynasty, stamped it with his own personal genius.

Art in general was declining, but not the art of the man who designed the decoration of these walls ; while the portion of the temple which is covered with inscriptions of the succeeding Ramses II. shows the decline in a marked degree. The reigns of Seti and that of his son were both long ones, so there may have elapsed some forty or fifty years' interval; but it was a sad falling off in so comparatively short a time.

The reliefs of Seti are slightly higher than those in Hatshepsu's temple at Thebes, but the increased size of the figures may partially account for this. Probably all were intended to be coloured, as a certain number of them are; but as time has served so much of the coloured work badly, perhaps it is fortunate that the majority still remain as they left the hands of the sculptor. I have chosen an illustration from both series. In one, where the hue has only been acquired through the discoloration of the limestone, Seti is bringing an offering to Osiris, a fragment of whose figure is seen to be left, and of the coloured series I chose the relief representing Seti being nursed by Isis. The modelling appears to greater advantage in the former, as the broken colour in the latter interferes with the light and shade. I restored the faces of the goddess and that of the young king, as the subject would otherwise have hardly been intelligible, and covered up ugly scratches that interfered with the design. The blues and greens are nearly gone and the blacks have quite disappeared, while the reds and yellows are nearly as strong as when first put on; we cannot therefore judge fairly of the decoration as a scheme of colour, but the design makes it rank among the great things that art in any age has produced. Now that they are exposed to the sun and to what little rain falls in Upper Egypt, they will probably lose more in one year than during the centuries they lay buried under the sand.

The original roofing-stones served as a protection; but without going so far as to restore these, it is a pity that some means are not used to preserve what colour remains. In dynastic times the pigments were protected by a varnish, which is still seen in places where neither the sun nor the occasional shower can reach it. Whether it would be better to give the colour here a dull varnish or to board in the roof is a matter to consider. Apart from the colour, the actual life of the stonework would be lengthened, for the changes of temperature as the midday sun strikes full on these reliefs must be very great, and is bound to act on the surface of the bruised stone.

This temple, being erected near the supposed grave of Osiris, is dedicated to the god of the nether world, and to his goddess Isis and their son Horus. The honouring of this triad was the subject the artist had to represent in these reliefs, not forgetting to show forth the special favour in which Seti stood,—even to usurping the place of the infant Horus. We see the King in different

Walter Tyndale

surroundings on the north wall of the hypostyle hall at Karnak. He is represented there as a warrior smiting a Libyan chief, and the vigorous battle scenes of which this is the chief incident probably served as a model for all the warlike scenes we find on the Ramesid temples later on.

There is some beautiful work still visible on the ruined walls of Seti's mortuary temple at Kurnah, and the grandeur of design of the great rock temple at Abu Simbel, which is known as a Ramses II. work, was designed during the reign of that Pharaoh's illustrious father. We find all the three forms of wall decorations used during Seti's time. These low reliefs at Abydos are the most beautiful; but the relief *en creux* was also much used, and with fine effect; that is, the background is not cut away, but the outline is incised, and the relief is within the depth of the incision. A very beautiful example of this is in his tomb at Thebes, where the young king is represented making an offering to the image of truth. This same tomb is also richly decorated with unrelieved wall painting.

After a few days at Abydos, a visitation of the 'khamsîn' made the place almost as unbearable as I had found Dêr el-Bahri. This wind gets its name from the Arabic word meaning "fifty," for it is during that number of days, from the beginning of April, that Egypt is liable to it. It is also known as the 'simoom.' The rising temperature, a change in the colour of the sky from blue to grey, and a stillness in the air, prepares us for its coming. This absence of any air stirring may last some time; the grey sky turns to a yellowish hue in the south, and a preliminary hot puff or two tells us that we are in for it. A long blast of hot air, as if the gates of the Inferno opened, now follows. It picks up the sand as it moves across the desert, and the distance is lost in a yellow fog. I have tried to paint the effect, but could not lay on a wash of colour, so rapid was the drying. Palette and sketch had surfaces like sand-paper before I could get a second wash ready, if my board faced the wind, and if I faced it myself I was blinded with the sand. I hope to try it again but not on the spot. The only way for a painter is to treat the 'khamsîn' as he would a wet day in England, and devote his time to doing the hundred and one things indoors that a long spell of fine weather has made him put off. One asks oneself how one will be able to stand May or June if it is as hot as this in April. I have, before now, packed up all my warm clothing during an early simoom, to send them home by *petite vitesse*, but have thanked goodness a couple of days later that they had not gone off, as a change in the wind has made me hurry to get them out again. When it blows from the north once more its bracing effect puts one in such good spirits that even the fear of a return of the enemy does not damp them ; one finds that one has not suffered in vain, for that plague of Egypt, the flies, will have very much abated ; and the hot wind has also thinned out the tourists, while those yet remaining regret that they were somewhat premature in securing their berths on home-bound steamers. April in Egypt is never spoilt by rain, and whether it is a paradise or an inferno during that month is determined by the quarter from which the wind blows.

I returned to Luxor by a night train as I did not like facing the ride across the cultivation till the sun had gone down. Dêr el-Bahri had cooled down a bit when I reached it the next morning. The excavations were over and every one had left but Currelly, who was seeing to the packing of the detachable bits of Mentuhotep's temple, previous to their going to London. The Hathor cow of the previous year, that had been acquired by the Cairo Museum, was accepted by it as a sufficient share of the finds to allow of all that had turned up this winter to fall to the share of the Egyptian Exploration Fund. My personal luggage was soon packed and sent on a camel to the river's edge opposite Karnak, where my friend Nicol's dahabiyeh lay. I was sorry to leave Currelly alone in this furnace, with tons of fragments still to pack, but my time was drawing to a close, and Karnak must figure in this book.

To get on to a clean dahabiyeh after the dust and heat of Dêr el-Bahri was indeed a joy. I look back with the greatest pleasure on my stay in the camp, a sojourn which lasted over five months, and its breaking up in dust and heat, in a confusion of packing-cases, empty tins, and broken 'antikas' not worth the transport to England, is not the phase that I shall store up in my memory to enable me to recall the happy time I passed near Hatshepsu's temple.

When we reached Karnak my friend Erskine Nicol moored the *Mavis* within five minutes' walk of the great temple. Howard Carter had given me a letter of introduction to M. Legrain, who has superintended the excavations there, and who must have a more intimate knowledge of Karnak than any man living; and my first morning was spent with this genial Frenchman and Nicol in "doing" the various temples enclosed in this great area.

I had been there several times before, but had only a confused idea of this stupendous mass of ruins. M. Legrain kindly told us the story of Karnak, and pointed out the growth of this city dedicated to Ammon. From foundations of the twelfth dynasty we traced its history until the time of Our Lord, a period extending over two thousand years. There are also some remains, dating from archaic times, which would double that lapse of time; but as we are only treating of such buildings as lend themselves to pictorial representation, we shall leave these earlier foundations to the archæologist. M. Legrain began life as an artist, and went through the *École des Beaux Arts*, therefore his artistic temperament, together with his knowledge of the place, led him to take us to points of vantage from whence the ruins were seen at their best.

The approach from the Nile, passing through the avenue of ram-headed Sphinxes, is the best to take in order to get the finest impression of the great structure that dominates this vast area of ruins. We enter through the gigantic portal erected by one of the Ptolemies ; this is the first main pylon. Its size is impressive, but its beauty or interest need not detain us long. The great court we enter prepares us for greater things to follow. One standing column with calyx capital attracts us more than anything else. The statue which it probably once supported is gone, and of its nine fellows that formed a double row in the centre of the court nothing remains but the pediments and some broken shafts. As we approach it, it is relieved against the ruined pylon of Ramses I., its beautiful capital clears the ruinous background, and stands boldly against the blue sky. The Ethiopian Taharqa is said to have raised these colossal columns during the twenty-fifth dynasty, a period which was the dawn of the last renaissance of what is most beautiful in Egyptian art.

Little is recorded of Ramses I., whose pylon we now pass through to enter the great hypostyle hall which his son Seti I. erected and his grandson the second Ramses completed. On first entering this great hall, with its 134 columns, one is filled with something of the awe that the first sight of the Great Pyramid inspires ; but here a highly advanced art has aided the brute force required in the construction of this monumental work. Enough remains to help one to reconstruct in imagination the effect the complete building must have produced ; and as it stands now it may be considered the grandest ruin in the world.

It would be impossible to attempt to give, with my unpractised pen, the impression of these colonnades which I have been able inadequately to give with my brush. The illustration depicts the double row of columns that supported the roofing-stones of the nave. A hundred and twenty-two such columns supported the two aisles. These being shorter than the central ones, it allowed of a double row of clerestory windows, which served to light the whole of the interior. The wall space pierced by

these windows rises from the roofing of the innermost rows of columns that support the aisles. What we will term the nave, for lack of a better term, forms in itself three great aisles. The less lofty ones to the right and left of it are each supported by seven rows of columns, which, with the outer walls, each form seven lesser aisles.

The effect of these 134 columns is most imposing; but the girth of each one is so great that their bases cover a very great proportion of the flooring of the interior. Whether this be architecturally right I should not like to assert, but the effect it produces is grand in the extreme. That it takes six men with outstretched arms to span one of these colossal columns in the nave may give some idea of their girth; their height is 69 feet, and the abaci and blocks of stone that support the roof make the total height of the exterior of this nave 78 feet. The architraves above the aisle columns rise to about the height of the shafts of the centre ones. Some of these had fallen seven or eight years ago, and it was interesting to hear from M. Legrain of the manner in which he raised them and replaced the huge blocks of stone that surmount and tie the colonnades. The means he used differed in no wise from the means that were at the disposal of Seti's builder. He would pile up earth till he reached the height of the missing stone, and form a sloping causeway up which the block would be hauled with the aid of tackle and rollers, and as this earth was moved from unexcavated parts of the temple near at hand, this labour served a double purpose. As labour is cheap during certain months of the year, he assured me that it was a less expensive procedure than the use of cranes and engines would have been. There is an enormous amount of this work still to be done. Many of the aisle columns are still buried nearly up to the spring of their papyrus bud capitals. Many of the roofing stones were probably used by the Ptolemies when they added their quota to the glory of Ammon or of some other Theban god. All the central columns, and most of the shorter ones, are inscribed with figures or cartouches of Ramses II.'s time. The much more beautiful work of Seti is seen on the inner side of the pylons that enclose the hall, east and west, and on both sides of the north wall. The few columns that still show the work of this Pharaoh make one regret that he did not complete this hall. His handicraft is all in the delicate low relief that recalls the work we have seen at Abydos, and which there contrasts so much to its advantage with the work of his son.

Leaving the hypostyle hall by the door in the north wall we can study the series of reliefs that depict the victories of Seti during his campaign in Syria, and, interesting as these are as an historical record, they are invaluable as a work of art. They are the great masterpieces of all the battle scenes, depicted from the rise of the new Empire till the conquest of Egypt by Alexander. The innumerable portrayals of a Ramses slaying a barbarian, repeated until one is ready to cry, "Hold ! enough !" were probably all inspired by this great work of art.

Re-entering the hall, we pass again through this forest of columns, and quit it at its eastern entrance through the pylon of Amenophis, or Amenhotep III., as we have been calling him. This older part of the temple of Ammon is in such a ruinous condition that, without the help of Legrain, it would have been difficult to know where we were. The two obelisks of Thothmes I., only one of which is standing, and a pedestal of a vanished colossal statue front the early eighteenth dynasty temple, which at that time had no buildings to mask it from the river. The pylon of Thothmes is now no more than a shapeless heap of stones. The second pylon, of which even less remains forms the eastern side of a narrow colonnaded court, nothing of which now stands, save the great obelisk of Thothmes' extraordinary daughter, Hatshepsu. Her unloving spouse, the third Thothmes, had encased the lower half with sandstone walls, which have since fallen down, and we can now see this pink granite monolith in its entirety. It is the finest obelisk in Egypt ; just under a hundred feet in height, and its estimated weight, according to Professor Steindorf, is 3,673 tons. Marks of the Thothmosid feuds are visible on the polished surface of the stone, also those of the religious revolution of Ikhnaton, where the figure of Ammon had been effaced, to be restored during Seti's reign, when the worship of that god was firmly re-established. Beyond this, the fifth pylon starting from the river is another colonnaded court of Thothmes I., flanked by Osiride figures; and passing through yet another pylon, we enter the forecourt of the sanctuary. The granite gateway of the last and smallest pylon has some beautiful work inscribed on its sides, with characteristic figures of Nubian and Syrian prisoners taken by the third Thothmes. The same Pharaoh erected two granite pillars in this court, the lily of Upper Egypt, on the southern one, stands in high relief and faces the midday sun ; while on the northern face of the second we see the papyrus of Lower Egypt. I took the accompanying illustration from one of the ruined apartments of Queen Hatshepsu which lie on the north and south sides of the sanctuary. The mutilated statue of Thothmes III. has been placed in the dilapidated boudoir of his half-sister and queen. Above rises the

granite sanctuary that Philip Arrhidaeus erected long after this ill-mated couple were laid to rest. It stands on the site of an earlier chamber, and when Philip erected it, much of the eighteenth dynasty temple was in a partially ruinous state. Late as this work is, it is one of the remaining gems of Karnak. Much of the original colour yet remains, and the granite of which it is built has a lovely hue. The inscriptions, cut as they are in so hard a material, are, in places, as sharply defined as ever they were. The interior walls are perhaps more beautiful still. The prevailing colour of the scenes is a malachite green on the pink background of the stone. The illustration being so much reduced from the original water-colour drawing, it is difficult to follow the inscriptions on the south wall that are represented. Here they are mostly picked out in red, and the conventional colouring of the hieroglyphs and the personages have been a good deal modified to suit a selected scheme of colour ; an artist's licence which would not have been allowed when the rulers of Egypt were more in sympathy with their gods. To the left we see the lily of Upper Egypt on Thothmes' truncated pillar, and above this Hatshepsu's great obelisk arises. The remaining clerestory window of the great hypostyle hall is just visible in the distance, and the ruined towers of the last pylon we have passed, break the remaining part of the sky-line. A flight of steps cut out of one block of stone seems still to puzzle the archæologists. It is very similar to the staircase of the altar of sacrifice in Hatshepsu's temple at Dêr el-Bahri, and it is possible that the same queen may have erected one here.

All we see here takes us, in successive stages, from the consolidation of the New Empire to the time when Egypt had fallen under the rule of the Greeks.

To the east of the sanctuary little but the foundations remain of the twelfth dynasty temple. The lapse of time between these relics and the building of Seti's great hall would embrace our own history from the period of the Norman conquest to the present day. Yet Seti is no modern, for the Pharaoh of the oppression, referred to in the first chapter of Exodus, is identified with his successor.

CHAPTER XVIII

More About Karnak

Beyond this site of the Middle Empire temple, and in alignment with those that we have seen, stands the colonnaded hall that precedes the sanctuary of Thothmes III. Working our way through the ruins, we find that this hall is merely a part of a vast temple, but it is neither awe-striking nor even imposing after seeing the work of Seti; though, were this the only building in this great enclosure, it might be both. The roof is supported by thirty-four square pillars and two rows of columns. The latter are more extraordinary than beautiful; for the inverted calyx capitals, and the downward tapering of the shafts, give them a topsy-turvy look that is not pleasing. Much of the inscribed work is beautiful, but time has dealt badly with it. In a chamber to the north of the ruined sanctuary the walls are covered with reliefs of plants and animals that Thothmes is said to have brought back from Syria. They are drawn with the sympathetic feeling for form which characterises the work at Dêr el-Bahri. The four columns that supported the roof of this room are in good preservation and are of the clustered papyrus type, with budded capitals.

After we had scrambled over the girdle wall of this temple, M. Legrain conducted us to a modest little shrine that he had lately unearthed at the extreme east of the great enclosure. It is fortunate that Legrain is an artist as well as an Egyptologist, for anyone not keenly alive to the beauty of the damaged reliefs on the walls might have lost us a very precious example of the twenty-fifth dynasty work. He told us that Shabako, the first of the Ethiopian kings, erected the little temple ; the reliefs were in a sad state of repair and quite gone in places where the sand-stone surface had disintegrated, but, "I think I can show you something you will like," he said, as he took us into an inner chamber and pointed out a relief of a Pharaoh presenting an offering to an almost obliterated god. The original colour is nearly gone, but what remains harmonises beautifully with the sandstone that it is laid on. As we got more accustomed to the subdued light, the beauty of the design disclosed itself, and we became less aware of the disfiguring joints in the stones. The Pharaoh is probably a successor

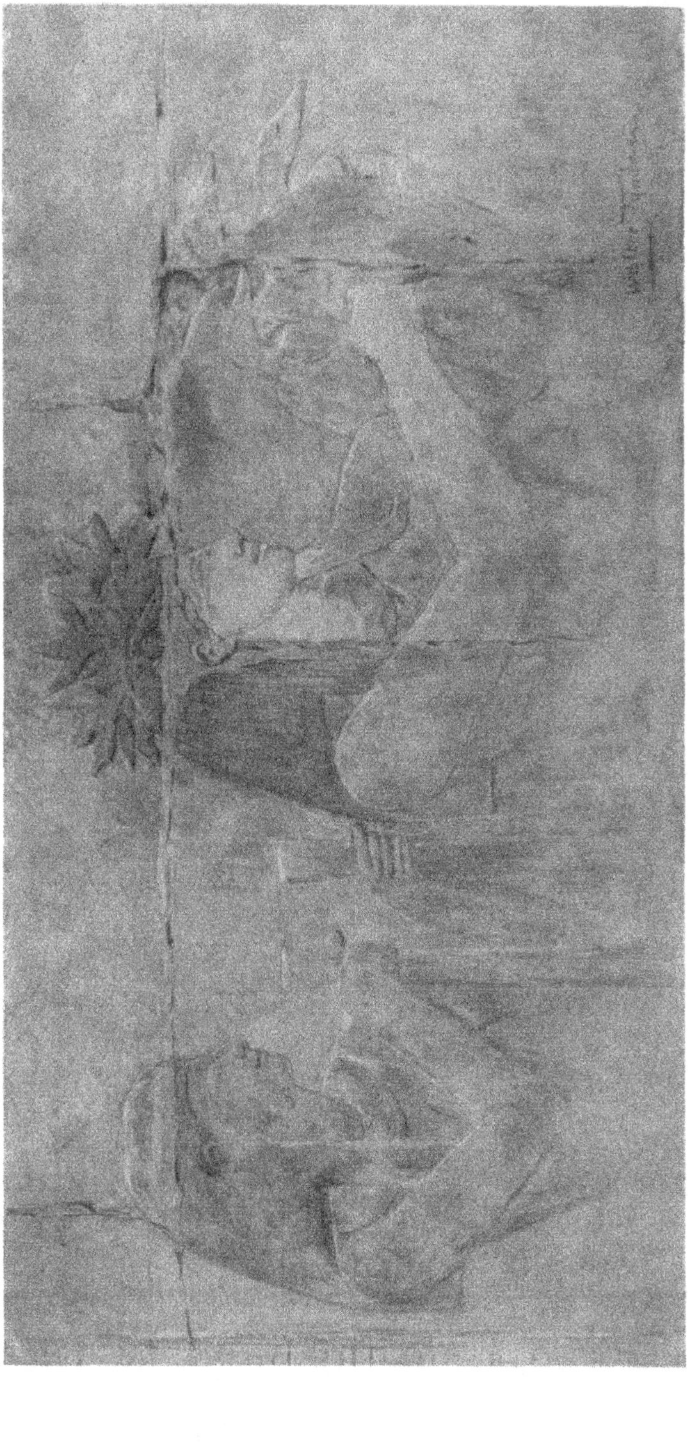

of Shabako Taharqa (the Tirharkah of the Scriptures) ; at any rate, I would prefer not to believe that this beautiful creature is the ruffian who burned to death his fallen enemy Bokchoris. That so fine an art could have been resuscitated during the rule of these Ethiopians is amazing.

It was difficult in the short time I had at my disposal to do anything like justice to my subject, and it has not lent itself very well to the necessary reduction and reproduction of the colour process. The undulating lines of the arms carry the eye to the right of the illustrations, beyond which is the object of adoration. The birds that are being offered to the god are barely traceable on the wall, but how prettily they fill the space. The leading line of the composition here stops short, and the heads of these birds send the eye of the beholder away from the king to the god he wishes to propitiate. Could any crown be more beautiful than that of the lotus flowers which the young Pharaoh wears ?

The little chapel that holds this faint echo of a supreme style of decoration is fortunately kept locked, and thus safeguarded against the fiend who sees nothing more in a work of art than a good background for his name.

The standing monuments and the interesting relics scattered about this great enclosure would more than fill a volume. To appreciate Karnak one must live in its proximity. During the three weeks I spent with Nicol, while the *Mavis* lay under the bank near the great temple, our time was too much occupied with painting to allow of our studying the place as much as we should have liked. So far, the reader has only accompanied us through the series of temples dedicated by succeeding Pharaohs to the worship of Ammon, and much that could be told of these is precluded by the limits of space.

Tucked under the north girdle wall stands a little temple erected by Thothmes III. to the Memphite god Ptah, which was added to under the Ptolemies. Towards evening the shadow of the great temple spreads over the intervening waste, and the sun-lit columns of this chapel rise up from the pearly-grey foreground. The russet colour of the embankment receives the golden hue of the capitals, and is in its turn relieved by a group of palms beyond the enclosure. It is a pretty subject, but at this time of day subjects are not hard to find. When the white light of the midday sun beats down on the vast mass of grey ruins through which we have wandered, a lack of colour makes it hard to treat pictorially, except in black and white.

M. Legrain conducted us to this chapel of Ptah,

and the heat and blinding light of the early summer sun made us long to get within its shade. Passing through two roofless courts, we entered a small covered chamber and almost ran against the statue of the lion-headed goddess Sekhmet, before our eyes had got used to the darkness of her abode. She is a magnificent creature, and one is thankful that she has not been grabbed up by some museum, but is allowed to stand where Thothmes placed her. Legrain told us that he found her here a few years since, but broken into some sixty pieces. Fortunately, none were missing, so he was able to piece her together with infinite labour, and he has been allowed to retain her here in her suitable surroundings. This lion-headed Goddess of War is awe-striking as she appears in the gloom of this chamber ; but I have studied her presentment in other lighting, when a certain look of dowdiness has replaced the awe-inspiring appearance which she had here. Perhaps a slight likeness to a lady pew-opener, whom I remember, may have helped this disillusionment. Something in her headdress reminded me of bonnet strings, and the sun-disk gradually changed into that emblem of perpetual widowhood, the crape bonnet, which I cannot dissociate from lady pew-openers.

Leaving Sekhmet to keep guard in this shrine of Ptah, we worked our way back to the central court of the temple of Ammon, and, crossing this, we proceeded to inspect the ruins on the south side. It seems more difficult to trace the plan here, and the reason for the four pylons that succeed each other in the three or four hundred yards until we reach the girdle wall of the enclosure. Thothmes III. and Hatshepsu are responsible for the first two, and the two further ones, which are somewhat out of the parallel with the great temple, were erected by Haremheb, the founder of the nineteenth dynasty. The base of the left wall which connects the ruined pylon of Thothmes with the temple, is inscribed by Merneptah. The eternal slaughtering of Syrians in which Ramses II., Merneptah's father, took such delight, is here carried on by the son, but what most concerns us is the artistic relation they bear to the inscriptions of his grandfather, Seti I. and the yet older work of the eighteenth dynasty.

By nature an unwarlike people, the art of the country seemed more in sympathy with peaceful subjects; and the wars of the Thothmes were not recorded in great battle pieces; an offering of the spoils of victory to Ammon seems a sufficient pictorial record, but when Seti I. drove back the Semitic tribes who had invaded his Asiatic dominions and who were becoming a serious danger to Egypt itself, the art of the country

seemed to wake up to the importance of these victories, and left us that grand memorial which we have seen on the north wall of the hypostyle hall. During the long wars of Ramses II., temples seemed built to form wall spaces on which to record the warlike deeds of the Pharaoh. Times out of number is he portrayed holding some poor creature by the hair, and preparing to strike his head off. The same subject, treated *ad nauseam* at the command of this vainglorious man, must have had a paralysing effect on the artist's work, and a marked decline is visible, which continued during the reign of his son Merneptah. Some great artists doubtless remained after the close of Seti's reign; and where their work was congenial, and where they were probably allowed a free hand, great works of art were produced. There is much to be admired in the Ramesseum at Thebes, and the rock-cut temple of Abu Simbel is perhaps the finest monument of its kind that the world has ever seen, while the little temple of Bet el-Walli in Nubia is also hard to beat; and one might give yet more instances of beautiful work, but, compared with that of Seti, and that of the previous dynasty, art in general was on the decline. This Merneptah is held by many to be the Pharaoh of the oppression, rather than Ramses II.; but the finding of his body in the valley of the Tombs of the Kings at Thebes is hard to reconcile with his being drowned with his hosts in the Red sea. Ramses may yet be the Pharaoh who "hardened his heart" and it is something to his credit that he had one to harden!

Beyond this ruined pylon of Thothmes III. we see some fine statues of that Pharaoh standing at the gateway of the pylon beyond. The pond below, which is once more being drained, served as a *cache* for a valuable find Legrain made here a short time ago. We must go to the Cairo museum to appreciate the value of his discovery. The figures standing here, fine as they are, are but those not considered worthy of being sent with the others to the famous museum. How this vast number of statues got to the bottom of this pond adds one to the many unanswered questions that are continually arising in this wonderful land.

This south part of Karnak is the most sketchable. The Sacred Lake, in the angle formed by these southern extensions, and the earlier part of the great temple, suggests many a picture. The view across the lake with the distant pylon of Nectanebo lighted with the afterglow, inspired Erskine Nicol to paint one of the best pictures that has yet left his easel.

Passing through the gateway of Hatshepsu's pylon, the battered statues of the Pharaohs which are relieved against it form a subject that time would not allow of my painting, but I live in hopes of still doing so. The lay of the land, with some pictorial trees, and the modest temple of Amenhotep II. in the space between Haremheb's two pylons, suggest many things to paint. We had many a stroll, between the lights, through the southern precincts of Karnak, which cover nearly as great an area as the temple enclosure itself. The scenes here lend themselves more to the landscape painter than to the architectural draughtsman, the relics of ancient monuments forming interesting incidents rather than the subject of the picture. Groups of palm trees, scrub, and coarse grass, break the oft-times dreary monotony of the grey stone.

An avenue of sphinxes of nearly a quarter of a mile connected the enclosure of Amenhotep III.'s temple of Mut with that of the great temple of Ammon. A lake shaped like a horseshoe encloses the south end of what remains of the shrine which that magnificent Pharaoh erected. These precincts are outside the area that is guarded by the antiquities department, and the *fellahîn* are free to let their sheep and goats find what pasturage they can here. The children bathe in this sacred lake and the flocks are driven here to water. Ram-headed sphinxes emerge here and there out of the soil, and some lion-headed goddesses cast their shadows on the waters. An indefinable charm is here that is generally absent from a show-place ; and, as I often wandered here in the cool of the evening, or by the light of the moon, I do not associate it with the heat and glare of the great temple enclosure ; which makes me liable to overestimate its charm compared with the more important monuments in its neighbourhood.

The temple of Khons, situated nearer the river, and north of that of Mut, is the best preserved of the three shrines which Ramses III. erected at Karnak. Though not built during the best period of Egyptian architecture, it is of especial interest from the fact of its being very nearly complete. Visitors are often taken here before seeing the masses of ruin in the enclosure sacred to Ammon. Seeing one temple in its entirety helps one to understand and reconstruct many of the fallen ones that one sees later on. So much of the roof remains that one gets the dim religious light wholly absent in the roofless remains of the earlier temples. The great portal of Euergetes I. stands a little way in front of this shrine of Khons, and an avenue of sphinxes built by the last of the Ramesides precedes it. An outlying part of the village lies near this handsome portal, and between the date palms arise some of the ram-headed sphinxes, though sometimes no more than a headless trunk shows above the soil. We were wont to pass here after our rambles round the temple of Mut, and the growing darkness made it difficult to find our way until we had cleared the palm groves and reached the open ground that separated Karnak from the Nile.

At length the summer heat obliged us to go north, and we drifted down the river ; feeling that we were only beginning to know something of these famous ruins and their possibilities for pictorial treatment.

CHAPTER XIX

The Temple of Dendera

Hot as it was, our progress down the Nile was most enjoyable. If the north wind blew hard enough to counteract the three or four miles an hour that the stream would take us during the calm, we would tie our boat up and start again at daybreak the next day. It seldom blows during the early hours, and as this is the coolest part of the day, we were generally up soon after the boat had started. An especially good subject would often keep us several days in one place ; but, should the wind veer round to the south, it was an opportunity not to be lost, and a satisfaction that the disagreeable 'khamsîn' could be turned to such good account. We had our studio on board, with a great accumulation of work to look over, and we were able to get on with this while slowly drifting with the stream. We would often tie up for the night while there was yet an hour's daylight ; and a walk with a gun would give us some exercise, if

it did not always help our larder. The notices not to trespass, that stare one in the face in the country at home, are absent here. One is as free to wander over the fields as to breathe the air; providing one takes care to injure no crops. As we were careful, and were able to distinguish between the wild pigeons that nest in the great columbariums and the tame ones of the villagers, and as no one ever objected to the former being shot, the peasants would help us to mark them. When well away from the centres where the Europeans congregate during the season, one finds a marked difference in the behaviour of the natives. The impertinence of the crowd at Luxor, who have come to look upon the tourists and visitors as a source of income that must keep them in idleness all the winter, is quite absent here. The eternal cry of *baksheesh* that sickens one in Cairo or Assuan, is seldom heard; and, as far as my experience goes, I have always found the *fellah* civil and obliging. Nicol, who has lived amongst them for many years, and speaks Arabic perfectly, was no doubt a great help in making our contact with the people pleasant. It is difficult for a Western to get at the character of an Oriental people, but with the help of my friend's experience I was able to form a better judgment of the modern Egyptian, and also to get some idea of how we appear in their eyes. Rumours at Luxor had reached us that the country was in an unsettled state ; the Denshaur incident had created some excitement in Cairo and the towns of the Delta, but the boatmen on the Nile and the up-river country folk seemed to know nothing about it. As long as the latter are left in safe possession of their plots of land, and are able to find a market for their produce, I do not think they trouble themselves much as to what nation has the most to say in the government of their country. The boatmen do not seem to have shared in the increased prosperity which has resulted from the British occupation, but they are naturally a peaceful lot of men, and they hardly realise what our position in their country is. The price of living has increased as a better market for the crops has been found, but owing to the competition of the railway, and other causes, the wages of the Nile sailors have remained stationary ; therefore, they are really worse off than ten or fifteen years ago. Their mania to be on the move seems unaccountable, for, as long as they could bask in the sun or sleep in the shade and get their wages, you would imagine that the longer the journey lasted the better it would suit them ; instead of which, should the wind not be dead against us, their faces would fall if we proposed to tie up a bit longer, even though moving might entail a long day at the oars. They were, of course, glad to stay when we got to some town to which any of them belonged ; but apart from that they always seemed anxious to be on the move. Fortunately for some of the crew, we tied up for a while at Tûkh, and one of the sailors who lived here brought us a savoury dish that this part of the river is noted for. It was very good, but too rich to partake of freely.

Kûs lies on the opposite side of the river, an important city in mediæval times, but now dwindled down to not much more than a country village. There is some charming landscape further down near Kuft, the ancient Koptos, and to wander about here, picking up a few birds to replenish our larder, fell in with our inclinations more than a tramp over to the ruins of a temple of Min. On the east bank of the river some *gayassa* laden with pitchers were awaiting a favourable wind to carry the Ballâs pottery down the river. The clay deposits are a little inland, but stacks of Ballâssa were piled up on the bank near the village that gives them their name. Our next stopping place was at a modest little village on the west bank opposite Keneh, our objective being the temple of Dendera. Nicol was searching for a good bit of Nile bank as a setting for a picture of "Watering the flocks," and signs were not wanting that this place was used for that purpose. The temple was three or four miles inland but there would be time to walk over to see it and get back before dark to the boat.

Egyptian landscape has a charm quite its own ; one may often see something in Palestine that may remind one of some familiar bit of country at home ; the Lebanon in places recalls similar views in other mountainous districts ; but the flat stretches of land, that are watered by the Nile, recall no other place, and belong to Egypt alone. No fences cut up the view and give it the look of a badly-drawn chessboard ; a change in the colour alone indicates where one crop may be more forward than another, or where one has been gathered in ; and the desert hills on the eastern and western horizons ever remind one that Egypt is "the gift of the river," for when the fertilising waters reach the limits of their level the fat land changes abruptly into a howling wilderness. Though still early in May, the harvest was nearly over, we would pass a yoke of oxen treading the corn near which some peasants, taking advantage of the breeze, were separating the wheat from the chaff. Flocks of sheep and herds of goats were being slowly driven over the stubble in the direction from which we came, to be watered at the Nile where the banks slope sufficiently to make the water accessible ; and Nicol could console himself that we had tied up at the very place for his subject, as we were told that the flocks were watered there every evening.

The scene of my operations now came in sight ; the dust was rising from the broken grey walls and the débris that usually surround a temple, and through this we could dimly trace the outline of the *façade*. The soil which partially covers these ruined habitations near the temples is of value to the *fellahîn*, and is sold to them by the Antiquities Department. It is in digging up the 'sebagh,' as it is called, that an occasional scarab or other 'antika' falls into the hands of these peasants, and in paying for the privilege of clearing away this dust the off-chance of a find no doubt enters into their calculations. We shall speak later on of a record find made during one of these operations. The donkeys that carry the tourists from river to temple during the winter are turned to account in the summer for carrying sacks of this manure from the temples to the fields. This dust has often obliged me to abandon a sketch. The space in front of the *façade* has fortunately been cleared, and allows us to appreciate its symmetry and fine proportions from a suitable distance.

The Greek influence is strongly felt in the

design. The temple was built during the early part of the first century, when Egypt became a Roman province; and though what we actually see now was erected by the Emperor Augustus, it ranks as a Ptolemaic and not a Roman edifice. The effect of this *façade* is very fine; the detail, as in most work of this period, suggests the skilled workman rather than the artist, but it keeps its place in this nobly designed building. It is difficult to compare this exterior with that of any temple of the eighteenth dynasty, as we have here the advantage of seeing the architect's elevation in its entirety; whereas in the earlier work so much is missing that one rather looks for picturesque bits than tries to study what their effect as a whole would be. Six Hathor-headed columns support the architrave and the bold concave cornice, and the winged sun-disk decorates the space over the doorway. The three columns at each side of the entrance are joined by a balustrade that reaches halfway up the shafts. The pronaos, or vestible, again compares favourably with those of the earlier temples, as the eighteen columns that spring from the floor still support the roof, and the capitals are partly lost in the shadow.

This temple can hardly be called a ruin, and the imposing effect of light and shade that was intended by the architect is seen to this day. The

eighteenth dynasty works may be finer, but their ruinous condition does not allow us to realise them as we can do in this and other Ptolemaic temples. In examining the wall inscriptions in detail one cannot help being struck by the falling off in the sculptor's art; but lost as they are in the great masses of light and shade they seem to serve their purpose. From the centre of the pronaos we look through the entrance to the hypostyle hall, and can just discern the last of the six columns, where they rise from the pavement to be lost in the shade of the roofing-stones which they carry. We see through the two antechambers beyond, and the increasing gloom in the perspective ends in the blackness of the sanctuary. We lit no candles, for the effect was all-sufficing. As we entered the hall our eyes got more accustomed to the gloom, and the small square openings in the roof admitted sufficient light to make the Hathor heads of the capitals perceptible. Passing through the two antechambers we reached the door of the sanctuary, where darkness reigned supreme. A corridor runs round this sanctuary and forms the egress for eleven chambers, of which the one immediately behind the sanctuary is known as the "Hathor room." This once contained a shrine and an image of the goddess; now it is the home of innumerable bats, and the batty odour that has replaced the scent of the incense soon becomes almost unbearable. Standing in the darkness of the sanctuary we can look right through to the entrance of the temple 200 feet away, and the blaze of light from the outside world obliges us to grope our way until our eyes are once more accustomed to the gloom. A small chamber to our left forms a passage into an open court, beyond which some steps lead up to a chapel, the entrance to which is formed by two Hathor columns. The jambs of the door butt against the shafts and nearly reach the capitals, while a balustrade connects these shafts with the walls. The sky-goddess, "Newt," is painted on the ceiling of the chapel, or kiosque, as it is sometimes called. I decided to return here the next day and set up my easel beneath this goddess; the peep through into the little court would, I felt sure, be a good subject under a more favourable lighting, and, as the chapel faces nearly north, it would be a comparatively cool place to work in. The staircase to the roof of the temple starts from just inside the small doorway in the illustration. A run up there to view the surrounding country in the setting sun, was well worth the climb, even though it meant finding the best part of our way back to the *Mavis* in the dark.

The Story of the Find at Karnak

The men still loading their donkeys with the septic dust around the temple recalled the story of the find which a *fellah* made some five years since while he was similarly occupied. We will christen him "Mahmoud" (if giving a Moslem a name can be called christening !). While filling his sacks to load his donkey, Mahmoud's shovel struck something more solid than 'sebagh,' and he unearthed a pot. This is not an unusual thing to do ; but an unbroken pot such as this is worth a piastre or two, so he proceeded carefully to disengage it from the soil. It being closed with a stopper, and its unusual weight, excited the man's curiosity. On opening it Mahmoud found that it was full of gold pieces, and, while still muttering a prayer of thanksgiving, he covered it over and carefully marked the spot, and again thanked "Allah" that he was working by himself, and would not have to divide the spoil with others. He returned here after dark to fetch away his hoard, and feeling about in the loosened earth he found two more pots, also very heavy for their respective sizes. He managed to get them back to his hut, where he feasted his eyes on the glittering contents. What were the riches of the Omdeh of the village compared to this heap of gold which Providence had sent to Mahmoud! The ambition of every *fellah* to own a bit of land instead of working the land of others was now within realisation. Though "Allah" had been gracious, it was more than He could expect that Mahmoud should part with his find, and only content himself with an inadequate reward. But to keep a secret was more difficult than Mahmoud had imagined; for half the pleasure of becoming rich is gone if one has to keep up the appearance of being poor. The Omdeh, meeting him a few days later, noticed that he was better dressed than usual, and chaffed him about looking such a swell. "Ah, don't you think that *you* are the only rich man in Karnak!" answered Mahmoud, as a boastful spirit got the better of his discretion. "What do you think of this?" he cried, showing the Omdeh a handful of coins; "and there are plenty more where these came from."

Seeing that they were not coins now current, the mayor of the village ventured on a few leading questions, and soon pumped the whole secret out of the peasant. For the rest of that day the old rascal schemed how he might get possessed of these gold pieces. The "two-faddah" copper coin in circulation among the poorer folk is about the size of a sovereign, and, brightly polished, might possibly pass muster for the more valuable coin in the dimly lighted hut of a *fellah* who was unaccustomed to handling the "guinêh." Anyhow, he would try it. That same evening the Omdeh proceeded to Mahmoud's hut, where he found our friend alone and keeping guard over his treasure. "You are lost, O Mahmoud!" he whispered; "the people in Luxor have got wind of your find, and it has got to the ears of the Mudir. A couple of soldiers are now on their way to arrest you, and you will lose all you have found, to say nothing of being beaten and locked up." Poor Mahmoud from the height of bliss now fell into the depths of woe. He grovelled at the feet of the Omdeh and implored him to help him out of the difficulty. "I am always, as you know, ready to stand by a fellow villager," answered the old humbug, "but you must do exactly what I tell you. The amount of your find is not known, so, when the soldiers come, produce only half, and I will buy from you the other half. A guinêh will I give you for each coin you sell me, and these I can secrete in my own house. One of my servants will warn me when the soldiers arrive in the village." Mahmoud was only too thankful to save so much from the wreck of his fortune and counted out 300 coins, for which he got in exchange an equal number of two-faddah pieces, which were dropped into a sack and carefully hidden away. The real gold coins were also put in a sack and stowed away beneath the Omdeh's galabieh, and both parties awaited the arrival of the soldiers.

The warning of the approach of these warriors was not forthcoming, as that was only a dramatic lie thrown in; but the tread of the two men was heard outside and Mahmoud turned livid with fear. The Omdeh stepped out and had a whispered talk; then, loud enough for Mahmoud to hear, he assured the soldiers that it was all right, and that there was no need for an arrest, for— "The man apprised me of his find as soon as he could and we have been counting the coins, which you can now give us the receipt for and take away." The old villain then produced a piece of paper which one of the soldiers stamped with his seal as a signature, and the pot with half of Mahmoud's gold pieces was handed out and taken away. "Now you may thank your stars that we have got over the difficulty as well as we have!" said the Omdeh. The poor *fellah* breathed again as he heard the soldiers move off, and rejoiced that anyhow he had 300 golden sovereigns still to the good; while the Omdeh now left the hut and, hurrying along, caught up the men with the pot of coins. Needless to say that these men were no more soldiers than the Omdeh himself,

W. Tyndale

but only two of the latter's servants, whom he had prepared to act the part. The whole of Mahmoud's haul was now taken to the old man's house, and in due course these Roman gold coins found their way to the various 'antika' shops in Cairo. Mahmoud dared not breathe a word of the trick that had been played on him, and had to content himself with the 300 little copper coins, which was all he got out of the find.

Now how far the Oriental imagination may have embellished this story I cannot say; and I must allow the reader to add as many grains of salt as he thinks fit.

As one story is liable to beget another, and while we are on the subject of finds, it may interest some to hear the palpable lie, that is rife amongst the natives, regarding the discovery of the predynastic body and tomb which is now in the British Museum.

The Story of the Predynast

Dr. Wallis Budge, the keeper of the Egyptian and Assyrian collections at the British Museum, was anxious to secure a complete set of the contents of a predynastic tomb. A Moslem dealer was commissioned to hunt one up if it was possible. He succeeded after a while in collecting a certain number of pots of the period, but was not able to get enough to satisfy his client, and there was yet the most important content of the tomb, namely, the body, to be found.

He heard that a Copt, who lived in the remote neighbourhood where he was prospecting, had discovered some tombs and might be able to supply him with what he wanted. "Here's my chance," he reflected, "between the two of us we may be able to furnish a complete set of tomb furniture, and should he not have a perfect body, we must see if we can't fake one up." The Arab hurried off to the Copt's dwelling while these pleasant thoughts were occupying his mind. The *kubti* lived in a lonely district at some distance from the cultivated land. Much might be done here without anyone being the wiser. The man was fortunately at home and ready to do a deal with his visitor. He had pots in plenty, but not a body worthy of the British Museum. Sinister thoughts laid hold of the Arab as he contemplated the spare figure of his host. To slay a Christian is a dangerous thing to do; but need he, as one of the faithful, let that prey on his mind, should there be little chance of his being found out? Evil thoughts soon lead to evil deeds. The Copt stooped down to examine his pots once more, and the Arab dealt him a blow on the back of his head. Seeing that his victim did not need a second, the Moslem stripped the body of its clothes and dragged it to a hollow in the desert. Here he trussed the poor Copt up in the position in which the predynastic folk were wont to lay out their dead, and trusted to the drying winds and the summer sun to dry the body up sufficiently to pass muster as a predynast. The next move was to collect the rest of the tomb furniture in the hut, load his donkey and get back to his home as quickly as he could.

Returning to the spot six months later, the Arab dealer found the defunct Copt done to a turn, got the body back to his shop, and sold it, with the pots, to the British Museum, where the reader can now inspect him whenever he likes.

That such lies as this one should gain credence among a people who are past-masters in the art of lying seems extraordinary. Where and how the contents of this predynastic tomb were found I could not ascertain, but as the truth would possibly be less entertaining than the fiction, I let the matter pass.

Nicol and I having both completed our work at Dendera, we made the most of an east wind to help us down the river. We reached Nag Hamâdeh before the wind shifted to the north. The Nile flows from east to west, from Keneh to Beliâneh, a little below where we now tied up—for it was difficult to settle down to work in the *Mavis* while we sped along this reach. Towns and villages seem almost to touch each other on our present northern bank. Spurs of the Arabian mountains advance in places to within a short distance of the river, and are often very fine in colour. The town of Deshneh rises out of the ruins of an ancient city. Fâu, which lies but a few miles lower down, looked extremely picturesque, rising as it does out of the remains of an ancient convent; but the wind was too favourable to make it advisable to stop for a sketch.

Nag Hamâdeh is a poor place for a halt, though, reaching it at nightfall, there was no help for it. A great dismantled sugar factory, and the railway bridge which crosses the Nile, are its chief uglinesses. We had told the Luxor postmaster to forward any letters here, so we sent one of the crew to call for them. A cablegram from home, which necessitated my getting back to England as fast as I could, lay awaiting our arrival. The 300 miles of the Nile between here and Benisuêf, that I had never sailed, had to be left undone. Fortunately I had been to Abydos, and I was able to console myself that I had seen every notable temple; but the site of Tel el-Amarna

and the tombs of Benihasan I had to leave unvisited.

As the night train took me past Beliâneh my pleasant stay at the camp across the plain at Abydos came back to me. Picturesque, but at the time fever-stricken, Girgeh could not be sketched from a safe place on the river; Zohag, with its famous red and white convents, must, God willing, be explored another time, together with many other Coptic buildings lying between this town and Assiut. Sleep soon came to the relief of the anxiety which the cablegram had produced, and I dreamt of the old convents past which the train was carrying me. I was fortunate enough to be able to sail from Port Said the next night, and in five days I was once more in London.

CHAPTER XX

Rosetta

Upsetting the chronological order of my travels I will ask the reader to accompany me to Rosetta, where I stayed for some time about ten years ago.

To avoid the heat of Cairo in July, I transferred my sketching field to the Lebanon, where I stayed sufficiently long to allow Damascus to cool down. While at the latter place I heard from my old friend Henry Simpson, who declared that Rosetta, where he was staying, was of all places in the east the most paintable he had ever struck. Rumours of the possibilities of Rosetta had reached me before, but being confirmed now by one whose appreciation of the picturesque is almost unique, I decided to proceed there as soon as my work in Damascus should be over. I caught a boat at Berût that coasted from there to Alexandria, and a five hours' journey in a very slow train took me from the last port to "El-Raschîd," as I was now taught to call Rosetta. More concerned with the pictorial possibilities of the place than with its accommodation, I had made no inquiries about the latter, but, had I looked into a Baedeker at the time, I should have noticed that he says " no inn " ; and as we had no boat and no tents I might have cried off. However, my friend met me at the station, and when I asked if we were far from the hotel, I thought I detected a smile when he told me the 'hotel' was within a ten minutes' walk. The queer old town looked very picturesque as we approached it in the dusk, but the queerest sight of all was the ramshackle old building which the proprietor called the " hotel." The lower stories were let out for the storage of any articles that would not suffer damage should the upper part fall in. There was not much in them except some heaps of charcoal and straw, under which the rats hurried when I looked in. Simpson warned me not to mount the stairs till the luggage had been carried up, and that it would be keeping on the safe side for only one at a time to ascend. It was still light enough to see that the staircase had evidently been an afterthought of the architect, who had run it up the side of the tall building in a zig-zag. It was covered in and looked like a square tower butting against the wall. A wide crack showed that staircase and hotel were about to part company, and I understood my friend's solicitude. I have often regretted that I do not weigh more than I do, but on this occasion I was pleased; and, judging from our fare, I was likely to remain a light weight as long as I stayed at the Hotel Karalambo! Having learnt, by the light of a tallow dip, where were the dangerous places in the floor of my bedroom, I stowed my traps where the rats were least likely to get at them, and sang out to Simpson to lead me to the dining-room, as I had eaten nothing but some unripe dates since breakfast. I heard, to my dismay, that we fed at the "bakkal" on the other side of the square; so, one at a time, we descended the dangerous staircase. A "bakkal" is a mixture of grocer shop, café, and restaurant, and this one having no bedrooms to spare, Karalambo, the proprietor, had rented the ramshackle building which we had just left, to accommodate any travellers who were brave enough to risk the staircase.

I was now introduced to Karalambo, who politely wiped the grease off his fingers on his nether garments, before shaking hands. A little Karalambo stared as only one unaccustomed to seeing guests could. Mrs. Karalambo then made my acquaintance; and before some steaming mess was ready for us, I had been introduced to most of the notabilities of Rosetta. This "bakkal" was the

W. Tyndale

meeting-place of the *élite*, and was crowded with Arabs smoking their 'narghilehs' and playing 'tric-trac.' I was glad of some food and did not stop to guess what I was eating, though I thought that some bits of carpet and india-rubber had found their way into the stew; but I found out afterwards that most of the meat was of that consistency.

The native doctor joined our table when the coffee was served; a bright, cheery fellow, who spoke English remarkably well. Though he had never left Egypt, his training for the medical profession had been much the same as if he had studied in London or Paris. He told us of his difficulties in contending with the prejudices of his co-religionists, and how the laws of Mohammedan society made it almost impossible for him to effect any cures amongst the women. He had got so far as to persuade some husbands to allow him to feel the pulse, or look at the tongue of a wife, through a slit in the curtain, but the disease had generally gone too far when he had been called in. He insisted on our dining with him the following evening, and left us at the bottom of the dangerous staircase. We found our way up, after relighting the candle several times, and turned in for the night. Happily, the rats did not keep me awake very long; and the bed had evidently not been slept in for so long that all live-stock had departed from it.

Rosetta came up to my expectations as a sketching ground, and Simpson was soon able to show me all the choicest bits. The bazaars were at their best ; some of the stalls were laden with fruit both from Syria and the surrounding country. Little savouring of Europe was seen here, and but few of the people had abandoned the native dress. Columns of old temples, or of early Christian churches, have been used to support a projecting story or to round off the corner of a building. The houses are built of long narrow bricks with wide joints between them ; they are of a rich brownish-red colour, a good deal of woodwork is seen, but the meshrebiya is ruder than in Cairo. The mosque of Sidi Sakhlûn is very extensive, and the vaulting is all carried by antique marble columns. Some of the smaller mosques, though very much out of repair, were none the less paintable. The fountains, schools, and baths, are all on a more modest scale than at Cairo, but there is nothing here to jar with their oriental character, as is so often the case in the larger city.

Simpson had done some admirable work in some of the little cafés, and I hope that before long Londoners may have an opportunity of seeing some of his water-colour drawings. The Rosetta period is, as far as I have seen, the best period of his art.

In spite of rough quarters, I made up my mind to stay on here as long as I could, for it was a gem of a place to paint in. I was able to hire a night-watchman to keep back the crowd while I was sketching in the baẓaars, and to ward off the dogs that are a nuisance here. The fruit stalls first attracted my brush. Oranges and lemons were in places heaped up in great piles to be sold by auction to the retailers; huge clusters of dates, baskets filled to overflowing with pomegranates, stacks of sugar-cane, and bundles of artichokes, gave one the whole range of the palette to play with. The lighting of these bazaars is very fine. The sun's rays are cut off by the matting and sacking which is spread over a rough kind of trellis, and the subdued light thus obtained is a rich golden brown. These subjects have to be painted very rapidly, and completed piecemeal after the effect is got; for the heap of lemons of to-day may give place to a pile of pomegranates to-morrow; and the view is also continually interrupted by the salesman and his customers. It is very exhausting work, and being at the time of the high Nile, the damp heat was very trying.

After a couple of days in the fruit bazaar, to start

a drawing in the quiet of a mosque was restful in comparison. A word from the Mahmoor (the governor of the town) to the Sheykh, set aside any difficulties there might have been as to our being allowed to set up an easel in the shrine of Sidi Sakhlûn. I was told the history of this saintly personage, but I have got it too mixed up with that of other great lights of the Mohammedan faith to dare to venture on giving it ; and his mosque was such a good sketching ground that I was prepared to believe in all his virtues, without question.

Another local saint lies beneath the dome of a mosque on the outskirts of the desert that separates Rosetta from Aboukir Bay. The sea breezes have silted up the sand to such an extent that the further side of the building is more than half buried, and the sand has to be continually cleared away on the front side to enable the worshippers to enter the portal, while the present cemetery is ten or more feet above the level of the floor of the mosque. I was making the drawing that is reproduced in the illustration, during the month of "Shanwâl," which succeeds the fast of Ramadân. It is customary then for the women to visit the graves of their deceased relatives and to deck them with palm branches. They would sit about this cemetery the whole day ; some would be bewailing the loss of a parent, while others, squatting in

groups, passed the time in talking about their neighbours' concerns.

I was confined for nearly a week to my garret in the Hotel Karalambo by an attack of ague fever. Our doctor friend was not only my medical adviser but nurse and caterer as well, and Mrs. Karalambo would be admonished by him if the beef tea proved more greasy than usual. His visits lasted the length of a large cigar. I would watch this as if it were an hour-glass, and when it had burnt down to the stump the cheery little 'hakim' would suddenly remember another patient, and be off, promising to come and smoke another weed later in the day. When I got on my legs again I was hardly up to working in Rosetta, especially on the poor fare that we got at the inn. The rainy season had commenced, and I found that the ceiling of my room had as many holes in it as the floor, and a shower-bath, though a delight at the proper season, is disturbing to a night's rest; also these jets of water would occasionally bring down a piece of plaster. One is liable to some heavy rains during the latter part of the autumn anywhere near the coast of Egypt, and I feared lest our staircase should slide away from the house. Therefore I decided to get away from Rosetta and return to Cairo. Simpson stayed on to finish his work, but joined me a few weeks later. I hope to have an opportunity of painting in this picturesque town again, either while camping out or living on a dahabiyeh ; for I am ten years older now, and less inclined to face the discomforts of living in a Greek " bakkal."

Some years after my stay in Rosetta a series of happy coincidences brought me back to within easy reach of it. My friend Simpson was spending the latter part of the summer on the houseboat of Mr. G. B. Alderson, a leading member of the English colony at Alexandria. " Noah," as he is called by his familiars, invited me to spend some time on his ark before starting for Upper Egypt. This " ark " was originally a gunboat but has been fashioned by its owner into a commodious and very comfortable floating habitation. It is moored in the bay of Aboukir opposite a villa which Mr. Alderson has built among the palms close to the sea front. Mrs. Richmond, a daughter of our host, occupied the house on the shore, where we repaired for our meals ; but our quarters for the night were always on the ark. I spent a delightful week in this earthly paradise. The weather was perfect, just hot enough to make us enjoy the sea breezes and the shade of the palm groves. Great clusters of dates hung from the trees, varying in colour from the palest gold to a rich brown and purple according to their exposure to the sun, and I was glad to have this opportunity of making some studies of these, for the date palm is never seen to perfection, except when this fine patch of colour appears beneath its fronds. Our genial host assured me that I had come a week too late to see them in their full splendour, as a good deal of the fruit had been gathered ; but enough yet remained for my purpose. Has one ever been shown over a flower garden when the proud owner has not regretted that one is a few days too late to see the roses at their best, or a few days too early to appreciate his lilies ?

The minaret that rises between the palms in the illustration is a modern erection and therefore has not been a silent witness of the historical events which took place round and about Aboukir. It has an interest of its own, however, as it is probably the only standing minaret ever built by a Christian as a gift to the people of another faith ; but I mildly suggested to my host that, as he was a member of the Church of England, *that* church might have been his first consideration ; however, on being told that he had built the church for the English at Ramleh, where there were plenty of rich members able and willing to support it, it was evident that a neighbouring Peter had not been robbed to pay an alien Paul.

Apart from these ethical considerations, this mosque is a great improvement to the appearance of the village, and is a proof, if one were needed, that it is not necessarily age which gives to earlier work its chief beauty. If the proportions be good, and the structure is in keeping with its surroundings, it will be beautiful from the very first ; but, on the other hand, should the proportions be bad, and the building ill-adapted to its site, age will never make it fine, but will at the best only help to disguise its imperfections. My excuse for such a platitude is that one is constantly hearing a building condemned as ugly simply because it is new, and one is recommended to see another with no virtues save that of age. It is as unfair to the architects who do good work now, as the collector of old masters is apt to be to a master who has the disadvantage of being alive.

But I had more to do in Egypt than to enjoy the shade of the palm grove and to study the colour of the fruit, delightful though the life was. I was therefore compelled to take leave of my kind host and hostess, and to wend my way to the station.

As I passed by the village the call to prayer directed my attention once more to the whitened minaret, and the last sound I heard was the sonorous voice of the muezzin, " Allah akbar, Allah akbar ! "

INDEX

INDEX

INDEX

INDEX

INDEX

INDEX

THE END

RICHARD CLAY AND SONS, LTD., BREAD ST. HILL, E.C., AND BUNGAY, SUFFOLK.

CPSIA information can be obtained
at www.ICGtesting.com
Printed in the USA
BVHW041406160419
545683BV00013B/170/P

9 781162 735078

Kessinger Publishing

ISBN 9781162735078

90000

9 781162 735078

Kessinger Publishing®, LLC
www.Kessinger.net